Best of

FRENCH

Comforts made simple

GARDEN *of* **GRAPES.**

Published by Garden of Grapes

Printed in the USA

First Edition: 2023

Introduction

I extend to you a warm and heartfelt welcome to the pages of "Bonne Appétit! - 100+ French Comfort Recipes You Can Master at Home." It is with great pleasure that I share this culinary journey with you, as we explore the essence of French comfort cuisine in a manner that demystifies its elegance and invites it into the heart of your own kitchen.

The theme of this cookbook is rooted in the belief that the best of French comfort can indeed be made simple and accessible for all. The kitchens of France have long been celebrated for their artistry, and in these recipes, we strive to unravel the secrets behind those delicious dishes that evoke warmth, nostalgia, and pure delight.

My inspiration for creating this cookbook has been a lifelong love affair with the rich tapestry of French cuisine. From the bustling markets of Paris to the quaint villages of Provence, each corner of France has its own unique culinary story to tell. I have been fortunate to learn from the masters and to observe the skill and passion that go into crafting the simplest of French meals.

In "Bonne Appétit!", you can expect to find over 100 French comfort recipes that have been handpicked to represent the very essence of this exquisite culinary tradition. These recipes are not just about taste; they are about the stories and memories that are created around the dining table, the joy of sharing a meal with loved ones, and the satisfaction of mastering a dish steeped in tradition.

Our aim is to guide you through this journey with ease, ensuring that the ingredients used are readily available and that the techniques are approachable for all home cooks. Whether you are a seasoned chef or a beginner in the kitchen, you will find these recipes to be both a source of inspiration and a reliable companion on your culinary adventures.

Within the pages of this book, you will encounter classic French comfort dishes, from hearty stews to delicate pastries, each designed to bring a taste of France to your table. We have also included tips, tricks, and techniques to help you gain confidence and expertise in your cooking endeavors.

So, join me in savoring the flavors, the aromas, and the traditions that have made French cuisine a global treasure. "Bonne Appétit!" is your passport to a culinary adventure filled with simplicity, elegance, and the purest of comforts.

Thank you for entrusting me with the pleasure of your culinary journey. May your kitchen be filled with the fragrances and flavors that define the best of French comfort food.

Coq au Vin Blanc
See page, 86

Cooking Philosophy or Approach

In the heart of every French kitchen, there exists a certain reverence for the art of cooking—a reverence that I have carried with me throughout my culinary journey. It is this very reverence that forms the cornerstone of my approach to cooking and that I hope to share with you in the pages of "Bonne Appétit!".

Cooking, at its core, is about celebrating the pure and natural flavors of ingredients. It is about taking the simplest of elements—fresh produce, quality meats, fragrant herbs—and coaxing them into a harmonious symphony of tastes and textures. It is a dance of techniques, patience, and intuition, where the ingredients themselves dictate the rhythm.

In this cookbook, you will find that my approach to French comfort cooking is rooted in tradition but embraces simplicity. It is about respecting the time-honored techniques that have shaped French cuisine for centuries while making them accessible to the modern home cook. The recipes here are designed to evoke the warmth of a French kitchen without the intimidation of complexity.

At the heart of French cooking lies the art of balancing flavors, and it is a theme that permeates every recipe within these pages. It's the delicate interplay of sweet and savory, the harmonious blend of herbs and spices, and the careful consideration of texture that defines the beauty of French cuisine. It's about the transformative power of a well-made sauce, the comforting embrace of a perfectly risen soufflé, and the joy of sharing a bottle of wine with friends over a home-cooked meal.

While "Bonne Appétit!" is a collection of recipes, it is also an invitation to explore the joys of cooking as an art form. It is an encouragement to experiment, to adapt, and to make each dish uniquely your own. It is a celebration of the connection between food, culture, and the stories we share at the dining table.

As you embark on your culinary journey through these recipes, I encourage you to embrace the ingredients with respect and care, to savor the process as much as the result, and to allow the spirit of French comfort to infuse your kitchen with its timeless charm.

In "Bonne Appétit!", you will find a reflection of my passion for the culinary arts and my desire to share the beauty of French comfort cooking with you. My hope is that these recipes not only fill your home with delectable aromas and flavors but also inspire you to create lasting memories around the table.

Tips for Successful Cooking

As we embark on our journey to master the art of French comfort cooking, I'd like to share with you some invaluable tips and techniques that will not only elevate your culinary skills but also ensure that each dish you prepare is a masterpiece of flavor and texture. These guidelines are rooted in the traditions of French cuisine, and they will serve as your trusted companions in the kitchen:

Quality Over Quantity: In the world of French cooking, ingredient quality is paramount. Opt for the freshest produce, finest cuts of meat, and the best quality dairy and fats you can find. Remember, the true essence of a dish begins with the ingredients you choose.

Master the Knife: A chef's knife is your best friend in the kitchen. Invest in a high-quality knife, keep it sharp, and practice your knife skills regularly. Precision in chopping and slicing will enhance both the presentation and taste of your dishes.

Mise en Place: This French term, meaning "everything in its place," emphasizes the importance of organization. Prepare and measure all your ingredients before you start cooking to ensure a smooth and stress-free cooking process.

Balancing Flavors: French cuisine is known for its balance of flavors. Always taste your dishes as you go and adjust the seasoning accordingly. A pinch of salt or a squeeze of lemon can make all the difference.

Homemade Stock: Whenever possible, use homemade stock in your recipes. It forms the foundation of many French dishes and imparts depth of flavor that store-bought options simply cannot match.

Searing for Flavor: The technique of searing meat or vegetables in a hot pan before slow-cooking enhances their flavor by creating a caramelized crust. It's a fundamental step in many French stews and braises.

Butter and Cream: French cuisine is often associated with these indulgent ingredients. Use them in moderation to add richness and flavor to your dishes, but don't overpower the natural flavors of the other ingredients.

Herbs and Aromatics: Fresh herbs like thyme, rosemary, and tarragon, as well as aromatic vegetables like onions, carrots, and garlic, are the building blocks of flavor in French cooking. Learn to use them judiciously.

Reducing Sauces: Reducing a sauce involves simmering it to concentrate flavors and achieve the desired consistency. This technique adds depth and complexity to many French dishes.

Patience and Practice: French cooking often requires time and patience. Embrace the slow simmer of a coq au vin or the delicate folding of a soufflé. Mastery comes with practice, and each effort is a step toward excellence.

Wine Pairing: Explore the world of French wines to enhance your dining experience. A well-paired wine can elevate a meal to a sublime culinary experience.

Respect Tradition, Embrace Creativity: While tradition is at the heart of French cooking, don't be afraid to put your own creative spin on classic dishes. Experiment, adapt, and make each recipe your own.

Remember, cooking is a journey, not a destination. The joy is in the process as much as in the final dish. With these tips as your guide, you're well on your way to mastering the art of French comfort cooking.

May your kitchen be filled with the delightful aromas and flavors of France, and may your culinary endeavors be a source of endless pleasure and satisfaction.

Seafood Gratin
See page, 95

Kitchen Essentials

To embark on your journey of mastering French comfort cooking, you'll want to ensure your kitchen is well-equipped with the essential tools and equipment. These kitchen essentials will not only simplify your cooking experience but also enable you to create the authentic flavors and textures that define French cuisine. Here's a list of indispensable kitchen tools and some tips on how to use them effectively:

Chef's Knife: A high-quality chef's knife is the workhorse of your kitchen. Keep it sharp and use it for slicing, dicing, and chopping ingredients. Precision in knife work is key to French cooking.

Cutting Board: Invest in a durable and spacious cutting board to provide a stable and sanitary surface for all your chopping and slicing needs. Consider separate boards for meats and vegetables to prevent cross-contamination.

Cookware

Heavy-Duty Skillet: A versatile skillet with a thick bottom is essential for searing, sautéing, and pan-frying. Stainless steel and cast iron are excellent choices.

Saucepan and Dutch Oven: These come in handy for simmering sauces, stews, soups, and slow-cooked dishes. Choose heavy-bottomed options for even heat distribution.

Baking Dish: You'll need this for casseroles, gratins, and roasting. Opt for a glass or ceramic dish that can go from oven to table.

Baking Sheet: Essential for baking pastries, bread, and roasting vegetables. Use parchment paper for easy cleanup.

Ramekins: These small, ovenproof dishes are perfect for individual servings of desserts like crème brûlée or soufflé.

Mixer or Stand Mixer: A mixer makes whipping, beating, and kneading a breeze, whether for delicate meringues or bread dough. A stand mixer with various attachments is a versatile choice.

Whisk: Use a whisk for emulsifying sauces, whipping cream, and incorporating air into batters. Choose a balloon whisk for better aeration.

Measuring Tools: Accurate measurements are crucial in French cooking.

Measuring Cups and Spoons: Invest in both dry and liquid measuring cups and a set of measuring spoons.

Kitchen Scale: For precise measurements, especially in baking.

Peeler and Grater: A peeler is handy for removing the skins of fruits and vegetables, while a grater is essential for zesting citrus, grating cheese, and nutmeg.

Sieve or Fine-Mesh Strainer: Use for sifting dry ingredients, straining sauces, and removing lumps from custards.

Mixing Bowls: A variety of mixing bowls in different sizes will help you prep, mix, and store ingredients conveniently.

Tongs: A pair of tongs with a comfortable grip is versatile for turning, flipping, and serving.

Wooden Spoon and Spatula: These gentle utensils are perfect for stirring delicate sauces and preventing scratching of non-stick cookware.

Knife Care: Regularly sharpen your chef's knife and practice proper knife skills to ensure precise and safe cutting.

Temperature Control: Learn to control heat by adjusting the flame or burner to achieve the desired cooking temperature in your cookware.

Balanced Bakeware: When using baking sheets or dishes, distribute food evenly to ensure even cooking and browning.

Proper Whisking: Use a gentle wrist motion when whisking to incorporate air without overworking the mixture.

Sieve Technique: When sifting dry ingredients, hold the sieve high above the mixing bowl to aerate the ingredients and ensure a lighter texture.

Measuring Accuracy: Measure dry ingredients by leveling off excess with a flat edge, and measure liquids at eye level in liquid measuring cups for accuracy.

Spatula Use: When folding ingredients, use a gentle, sweeping motion to maintain the desired texture.

With these kitchen essentials and tips, you're well-prepared to dive into the world of French comfort cooking. May your kitchen be a place of culinary creativity, and may the aromas and flavors of France infuse your dishes with the spirit of authenticity.

Tuna Noodle Casserole
See page, 19

Flavor Pairing Suggestions

French cuisine is renowned for its artful balance of flavors, and within its vast culinary landscape lies a world of possibilities when it comes to flavor pairings. As you embark on your journey to master French comfort cooking, consider these flavor pairing suggestions to inspire your culinary creativity and help you craft dishes that are truly remarkable:

Herbs and Proteins

Tarragon and Chicken: The anise-like aroma of tarragon pairs beautifully with the subtle flavors of chicken, creating a classic French combination.
Rosemary and Lamb: The robust, pine-like flavor of rosemary complements the rich and earthy taste of lamb.

Fruits and Meats:

Apples and Pork: The sweetness and tartness of apples contrast beautifully with the savory notes of pork, making it a classic pairing in French cuisine.
Cherries and Duck: The bold, sweet-tartness of cherries enhances the richness of duck dishes.

Citrus and Seafood

Lemon and Sole: The bright acidity of lemon juice and zest elevates the delicate flavors of sole or other white fish.
Orange and Salmon: The sweetness of orange pairs wonderfully with the richness of salmon, offering a vibrant contrast.

Wine and Food

Red Wine and Beef: A rich red wine sauce can complement the depth of flavor in beef dishes, such as boeuf bourguignon.
White Wine and Seafood: White wine, often used in seafood dishes, adds brightness and acidity to balance the brininess of seafood.

Sauces and Proteins

Béchamel and Ham: The creamy, white béchamel sauce harmonizes with the smoky, salty flavors of ham.
Hollandaise and Asparagus: The velvety texture and buttery richness of hollandaise sauce enhance the freshness of asparagus.
Cream and Savory: Creamy elements add a luxurious touch to many French dishes.

Crème Fraîche and Potatoes: The tangy richness of crème fraîche complements the earthiness of potatoes in dishes like gratin dauphinois.
Gruyère and Onion: Gruyère cheese and caramelized onions combine to create a delightful, savory pairing in dishes like French onion soup.

Mustard and Meats

Dijon Mustard and Pork: The sharpness of Dijon mustard enhances the flavor of pork, making it a classic French combination.
Grainy Mustard and Sausages: The texture and tanginess of grainy mustard add complexity to sausage dishes.

Nutty and Sweet

Almonds and Desserts: Toasted almonds are often used to add a delightful crunch and nutty flavor to French desserts like tarts and frangipane.

Cinnamon and Chocolate: The warm, aromatic spice of cinnamon complements the richness of chocolate in desserts and hot beverages.

Parsley and Garlic: A classic combination in French cooking, the freshness of parsley balances the pungency of garlic in many dishes.

Tomatoes and Goat Cheese: The acidity of tomatoes contrasts beautifully with the creamy, tangy flavor of goat cheese in salads, tarts, and quiches.
Spinach and Gruyère: Spinach and gruyère cheese pair wonderfully in savory pastries and gratins.

Chives and Butter: The mild onion flavor of chives complements the richness of butter, making it a classic pairing for baked potatoes and sauces.

These flavor pairing suggestions are just the beginning of your culinary exploration. French cooking encourages creativity and experimentation, so don't hesitate to mix and match ingredients to create your own delightful combinations. Trust your palate, and let your taste buds guide you in crafting dishes that capture the essence of French comfort cuisine.

May your culinary journey be filled with the joy of discovery and the satisfaction of savoring the harmonious flavors of France.

Chapter 1:
Classic Soups and Starters

4
servings

280 cal

15 min

French Onion Soup

Ingredients:

- 4 large onions
- 4 tbsp butter
- 1 tbsp olive oil
- 2 cloves garlic
- 1 tsp sugar
- 4 cups beef broth
- 1/2 cup dry white wine
- Salt and pepper to tasts
- Baguette slices
- Gruyère cheese

Indulge in a timeless classic. Originating in the bustling streets of Paris, this soup has won hearts worldwide. The slow-cooked onions in a rich broth dance harmoniously with toasted baguette and melted Gruyère cheese. Warmth in every spoonful.

Directions

1. Heat butter and oil, caramelize onions.
2. Add garlic, sugar, cook briefly.
3. Pour in wine, reduce.
4. Add broth, simmer.
5. Toast baguette slices, top with cheese.
6. Ladle soup into bowls, add cheesy baguette.
7. Broil until cheese melts. Serve hot.

Substitutions

Swiss cheese for Gruyère, vegetable broth for beef broth

6
servings

220 cal

20 min

Creamy Potato Leek Soup

Ingredients:

- 3 leeks
- 4 potatoes
- 2 tbsp butter
- 4 cups chicken brot
- 1 cup heavy cream
- Salt and pepper to taste
- Chopped chives for garnish

A velvety embrace from the countryside. Born from humble ingredients, this soup marries tender leeks and hearty potatoes. The delicate balance of creaminess and earthiness makes every spoonful a comfort-laden journey.

Directions

1. Sauté leeks in butter until tender.
2. Add potatoes, broth, simmer.
3. Blend until smooth.
4. Return to pot, add cream, season.
5. Simmer briefly.
6. Ladle into bowls, garnish with chives. Serve warm.

Substitutions

Vegetable broth for chicken broth

4
servings

180 cal

25 min

Tomato Basil Soup

A taste of the sun-soaked Provence. Bursting with the essence of ripe tomatoes and fragrant basil, this soup is a celebration of simplicity. Whether enjoyed hot or cold, it embodies the sun-kissed flavors of the Mediterranean.

Ingredients:

- 6 ripe tomatoes
- 1 onion
- 2 cloves garlic
- 2 cups vegetable broth
- 1/2 cup fresh basil leaves
- 2 tbsp olive oil
- Salt and pepper to taste

Directions

1. Blanch tomatoes, peel and chop.
2. Sauté onion and garlic in oil.
3. Add tomatoes, cook.
4. Pour in broth, simmer.
5. Blend with basil, season.
6. Return to pot, reheat gently.
7. Serve hot or chilled.

Substitutions

Canned tomatoes for fresh, dried basil for fresh

6
servings

250 cal

30 min

Beef Consommé with Mini Meatballs

Ingredients:

- 1 lb lean ground beef
- 1 egg
- 1/4 cup breadcrumbs
- 1 onion, 2 carrots
- 2 cloves garlic
- 8 cups beef broth
- 1 cup frozen peas
- Salt and pepper to taste

Elegance in a bowl, perfected through generations. This consommé showcases clarity, flavor, and love. Mini meatballs add a playful twist, making every sip a joyous revelation of tender meat and golden broth.

Directions

1. Mix beef, egg, breadcrumbs, season.
2. Form mini meatballs.
3. Sauté onion, carrots, garlic.
4. Add broth, bring to simmer.
5. Add meatballs, peas, cook.
6. Season, serve with love.

Substitutions

Ground turkey for beef, green beans for peas

4
servings

240 cal

25 min

Velouté de Champignons (Cream of Mushroom Soup)

Ingredients:

- 1 lb mushrooms
- 2 tbsp butter
- 1 onion
- 2 cloves garlic
- 4 cups chicken broth
- 1 cup heavy cream
- 1 tsp thyme leaves
- Salt and pepper to taste

A woodland embrace transformed into elegance. Velvety mushrooms dance in a creamy symphony, while a touch of thyme adds depth. This soup elevates the ordinary to the extraordinary, capturing the essence of comfort.

Directions

1. Sauté mushrooms in butter.
2. Add onion, garlic, thyme.
3. Pour in broth, simmer.
4. Blend until smooth.
5. Return to pot, add cream, season.
6. Simmer gently.
7. Serve hot, garnish with thyme.

Substitutions

Mixed mushrooms for regular, dried thyme for fresh

6
servings

280 cal

35 min

Lentil Soup with Smoked Sausage

Ingredients:

- 2 cups green lentils
- 1 onion
- 2 carrots
- 2 celery stalks
- 2 cloves garlic
- 8 cups chicken broth
- 1 lb smoked sausage
- 1 tsp thyme leaves
- Salt and pepper to taste

A rustic melody of earthy lentils and hearty sausage. Hailing from the French countryside, this soup sings with the flavors of tradition. The smoky depth of the sausage intertwines with tender lentils, crafting a symphony of comfort and satisfaction.

Directions

1. Rinse lentils, chop veggies.
2. Sauté veggies in oil.
3. Add lentils, broth, thyme.
4. Simmer until lentils tender.
5. Add sliced sausage, cook.
6. Season, serve warm.

Substitutions

Any variety of sausage, vegetable broth for chicken broth

4
servings

220 cal

40 min

Vichyssoise (Chilled Leek and Potato Soup)

Ingredients:

- 4 leeks
- 4 potatoes
- 2 tbsp butter
- 4 cups chicken broth
- 1 cup heavy cream
- Chopped chives for garnish
- Salt and white pepper to taste

A chilled whisper of luxury, straight from Paris. This creamy, dreamy concoction marries leeks and potatoes in a symphony of flavors. Served cold, it's a refined delicacy, a quiet reminder that elegance often lies in simplicity.

Directions

1. Clean and slice leeks.
2. Sauté leeks in butter.
3. Add potatoes, broth, simmer.
4. Blend until smooth.
5. Return to pot, add cream, season.
6. Chill thoroughly.
7. Garnish with chives, serve cold.

Substitutions

Vegetable broth for chicken broth

4
servings

320 cal

45 min

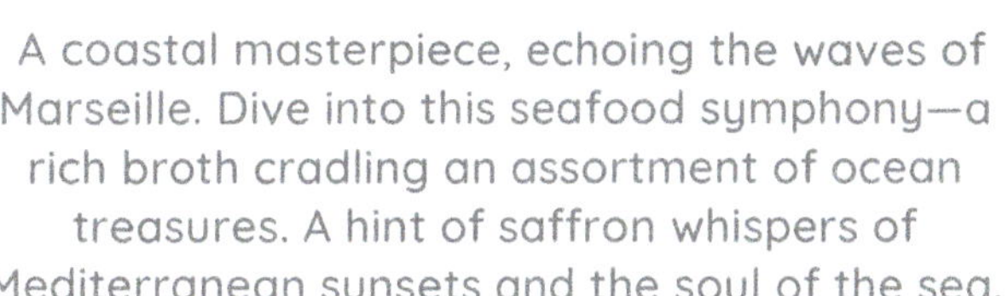

Provencal Fish Soup (Bouillabaisse)

Ingredients:

- 1 lb mixed fish and seafood (shrimp, mussels, fish fillets)
- 1 onion
- 2 cloves garlic
- 1 fennel bulb
- 1 cup diced tomatoes
- 4 cups fish broth
- 1/2 cup dry white wine
- 1/4 tsp saffron threads
- 2 tbsp olive oil
- Salt and pepper to taste

A coastal masterpiece, echoing the waves of Marseille. Dive into this seafood symphony—a rich broth cradling an assortment of ocean treasures. A hint of saffron whispers of Mediterranean sunsets and the soul of the sea.

Directions

1. Sauté onion, fennel, garlic in oil.
2. Add tomatoes, wine, saffron.
3. Pour in broth, simmer.
4. Add fish and seafood, cook.
5. Season, serve with crusty bread.

Substitutions

Any assortment of seafood, vegetable broth for fish broth

4
servings

200 cal

30 min

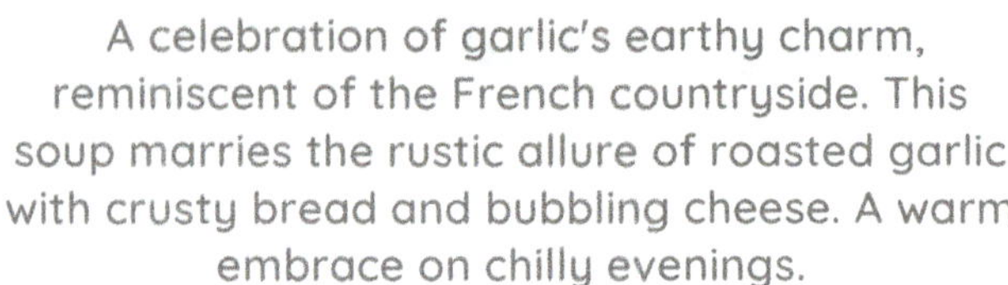

French Garlic Soup (Soupe à l'Ail)

Ingredients:

- 1 head garlic
- 4 cups chicken broth
- 2 cups stale bread cubes
- 1/2 cup grated Gruyère cheese
- 2 tbsp olive oil
- Fresh thyme leaves for garnish
- Salt and pepper to taste

A celebration of garlic's earthy charm, reminiscent of the French countryside. This soup marries the rustic allure of roasted garlic with crusty bread and bubbling cheese. A warm embrace on chilly evenings.

Directions

1. Roast garlic, squeeze cloves.
2. Bring broth to simmer, add garlic.
3. Toast bread cubes in oil.
4. Place bread in bowls, ladle in broth.
5. Top with cheese, broil until golden.
6. Garnish with thyme, serve warm.

Substitutions

Swiss cheese for Gruyère, vegetable broth for chicken broth

6
servings

180 cal

50 min

Chicken Liver Pâté with Baguette

Ingredients:

- 1/2 lb chicken livers
- 1 onion
- 2 cloves garlic
- 1/4 cup brandy
- 1/2 cup heavy cream
- 4 tbsp butter
- 1 tsp thyme leaves
- Salt and pepper to taste

Elevate your senses with this Parisian delight. A silky pâté, rich with the flavors of chicken liver and a touch of brandy. Spread it on a toasted baguette slice and let it transport you to the charming cafes of France.

Directions

1. Sauté onion, garlic in butter.
2. Add chicken livers, cook until pink fades.
3. Pour in brandy, flame gently.
4. Blend livers, cream, thyme until smooth.
5. Season, chill until firm.
6. Spread on toasted baguette slices, serve.

Substitutions

Cognac for brandy

Chapter 2:
Hearty Casseroles and Gratin

4
servings

320 cal

40 min

Chicken and Mushroom Casserole

Ingredients:

- 4 chicken breasts
- 8 oz mushrooms
- 1 onion
- 1 cup heavy cream
- 1/2 cup chicken broth
- 1 cup breadcrumbs
- 2 tbsp butter
- 2 tbsp olive oil
- Fresh parsley for garnish
Salt and pepper to taste

A symphony of flavors, baked to perfection. Tender chicken and earthy mushrooms mingle in a creamy embrace, crowned with a golden breadcrumb topping. This casserole captures the essence of comfort and elegance on a single plate.

Directions

1. Sauté chicken until golden.
2. Sauté mushrooms, onion in butter and oil.
3. Add cream, broth, simmer.
4. Place chicken in casserole dish.
5. Pour mushroom mixture over chicken.
6. Top with breadcrumbs, drizzle with oil.
7. Bake until golden.
8. Garnish with parsley, serve warm.

Substitutions

Mixed mushrooms for regular, vegetable broth for chicken broth

6 servings

380 cal

2 hours

Beef Bourguignon

Ingredients:

- 2 lbs beef stew meat
- 1 onion
- 2 carrots
- 2 cloves garlic
- 2 cups red wine
- 2 cups beef broth
- 2 tbsp tomato paste
- 1 tsp thyme leaves
- 1 tsp rosemary leaves
- 1 cup pearl onions
- 1 cup mushrooms
- 2 tbsp olive oil
- Salt and pepper to taste

A masterpiece born in the heart of Burgundy. This stew marries tender beef, red wine, and aromatic herbs in a slow-cooked dance. The result is a luxurious melody of flavors, each bite singing the praises of French comfort cuisine.

Directions

1. Sauté beef in oil, remove.
2. Sauté onion, carrots, garlic.
3. Add tomato paste, herbs.
4. Return beef, add wine, broth.
5. Simmer covered, then uncovered.
6. Sauté onions, mushrooms, add to stew.
7. Season, serve with crusty bread.

Substitutions

Any root vegetables for carrots, chicken broth for beef broth

6
servings

300 cal

1.5
hours

Gratin Dauphinois (Potato Gratin)

Ingredients:

- 4 lbs potatoes
- 2 cups heavy cream
- 2 cloves garlic
- 1 cup grated Gruyère cheese
- 1/4 tsp nutmeg
- 2 tbsp butter
- Salt and pepper to taste

Elegance and simplicity come together in this creamy creation. Layers of thinly sliced potatoes, infused with garlic and cream, create a harmony of textures. Baked to perfection, this gratin is a timeless celebration of comfort.

Directions

1. Preheat oven.
2. Slice potatoes and garlic.
3. Arrange layers of potatoes in dish.
4. Pour cream, seasonings, over layers.
5. Top with cheese, dot with butter.
6. Bake until golden and bubbling.
7. Serve hot, revel in simplicity.

Substitutions

Swiss cheese for Gruyère, milk for cream

6
servings

220 cal

1 hour

Ratatouille

Ingredients:

- 1 eggplant
- 2 bell peppers
- 2 zucchini
- 4 tomatoes
- 1 onion
- 2 cloves garlic
- 2 tbsp olive oil
- 1 tsp thyme leaves
- 1 tsp oregano leaves
- Salt and pepper to taste

A vibrant canvas of flavors, inspired by the fields of Provence. This vegetable medley dances with the colors of the rainbow—eggplant, peppers, zucchini, and tomatoes. Slow-cooked to perfection, it's a culinary masterpiece that captures the essence of summer.

Directions

1. Slice vegetables, sauté onion, garlic.
2. Layer veggies in dish, drizzle oil.
3. Season with herbs, salt, and pepper.
4. Cover, bake until tender.
5. Serve warm, let flavors sing.

Substitutions

Any variety of vegetables

4
servings

340 cal

2.5
hours

Coq au Vin

A tapestry of flavors, rooted in Burgundian tradition. This dish elevates humble chicken into a rich symphony of red wine, mushrooms, and pearl onions. A celebration of patience and culinary finesse.

Ingredients:

- 4 chicken legs
- 2 cups red wine
- 1 onion, 2 carrots
- 2 cloves garlic
- 1 cup mushrooms
- 1 cup pearl onions
- 1 cup chicken broth
- 2 tbsp olive oil
- 2 tbsp butter
- 1 tsp thyme leaves
- 1 tsp rosemary leaves
- Salt and pepper to taste

Directions

1. Sauté chicken in oil, remove.
2. Sauté onion, carrots, garlic.
3. Add wine, herbs, reduce.
4. Return chicken, add broth, simmer.
5. Sauté mushrooms, onions.
6. Add mushrooms, onions to chicken.
7. Simmer until tender.
8. Serve with crusty bread, savor each bite.

Substitutions

Any variety of mushrooms

6
servings

320 cal

1.5
hours

Quiche Lorraine

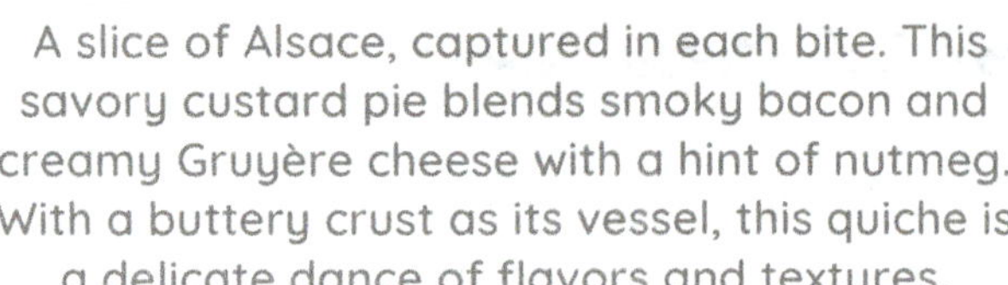

Ingredients:

- 1 pie crust
- 6 slices bacon
- 1 onion
- 1 1/2 cups grated Gruyère cheese
- 4 eggs
- 1 1/2 cups heavy cream
- 1/4 tsp nutmeg
- Salt and pepper to taste

A slice of Alsace, captured in each bite. This savory custard pie blends smoky bacon and creamy Gruyère cheese with a hint of nutmeg. With a buttery crust as its vessel, this quiche is a delicate dance of flavors and textures.

Directions

1. Preheat oven, partially bake crust.
2. Cook bacon, sauté onion.
3. Sprinkle bacon, onion, cheese on crust.
4. Whisk eggs, cream, nutmeg, season.
5. Pour over filling.
6. Bake until set and golden.
7. Let cool slightly, slice and serve.

Substitutions

Swiss cheese for Gruyère, milk for cream

6
servings

280 cal

45 min

Tuna Noodle Casserole

Ingredients:

- 8 oz egg noodles
- 2 cans tuna
- 1 onion
- 1 cup frozen peas
- 2 cups milk
- 1 cup grated cheddar cheese
- 1/2 cup breadcrumbs
- 2 tbsp butter
- 1 tsp thyme leaves
- Salt and pepper to taste

A humble yet satisfying melody of flavors. This casserole marries tuna, tender noodles, and creamy sauce. Topped with a crunchy breadcrumb crust, it's a comfort classic that brings generations together at the table.

Directions

1. Cook noodles, sauté onion.
2. Combine noodles, tuna, peas.
3. Make sauce with butter, flour, milk.
4. Stir in cheese, season.
5. Pour sauce over noodles.
6. Top with breadcrumbs, bake until golden.
7. Sprinkle thyme, serve warm.

Substitutions

Any variety of canned fish, any vegetables

6
servings

200 cal

1 hour

Vegetable Tian

Ingredients:

- 2 zucchinis
- 2 tomatoes
- 2 potatoes
- 1 onion
- 2 cloves garlic
- 2 tbsp olive oil
- 1 tsp thyme leaves
- 1 tsp rosemary leaves
- Salt and pepper to taste

A colorful celebration of the harvest. Layers of vibrant vegetables, kissed by olive oil and sprinkled with herbs, bake into a tapestry of flavors. This tian captures the essence of Provençal cuisine and brings summer to your table.

Directions

1. Preheat oven.
2. Slice veggies thinly.
3. Sauté onion, garlic in oil.
4. Layer veggies in baking dish.
5. Drizzle with oil, seasonings.
6. Cover, bake until tender.
7. Uncover, bake until golden.
8. Serve warm, taste the harvest.

Substitutions

Any variety of vegetables

6
servings

360 cal

2 hours

French Canadian Tourtière

Ingredients:

- 1 lb ground pork
- 1 onion, 2 cloves garlic
- 2 potatoes
- 1/2 tsp cinnamon
- 1/4 tsp cloves
- 1/4 tsp nutmeg
- 1/4 cup chicken broth
- 1 pie crust
- Salt and pepper to taste

A savory journey through French Canadian heritage. This meat pie boasts a filling of tender ground pork and aromatic spices, encased in a flaky crust. Each bite is a nod to tradition, a tribute to the flavors that define a culture.

Directions

1. Sauté pork, onion, garlic.
2. Add spices, potatoes, broth.
3. Simmer until tender, mash slightly.
4. Preheat oven.
5. Line pie plate with crust.
6. Fill with pork mixture.
7. Cover with second crust, seal edges.
8. Bake until golden.
9. Slice, savor the heritage.

Substitutions

Ground beef for pork, vegetable broth for chicken broth

4 servings

280 cal

1 hour

Ham and Cheese Gratin

Ingredients:

- 2 large potatoes
- 8 oz cooked ham
- 1 1/2 cups grated Gruyère cheese
- 1 cup heavy cream
- 1/2 cup breadcrumbs
- 2 tbsp butter
- 1 tsp thyme leaves
- Salt and pepper to taste

A symphony of comfort, adorned with smoky ham and creamy cheese. This gratin unites layers of ham and potatoes, bathed in velvety cheese sauce. With a golden breadcrumb crown, it's a dish that embodies the heart of home cooking.

Directions

1. Preheat oven.
2. Slice potatoes and ham.
3. Layer potatoes, ham, cheese.
4. Combine cream, thyme, pour over layers.
5. Top with breadcrumbs, dot with butter.
6. Bake until golden and bubbling.
7. Serve warm, taste the comfort.

Substitutions

Swiss cheese for Gruyère, milk for cream

Chapter 3: Comforting Main Courses

4 servings

300 cal

2 hours

Poulet Rôti (Roast Chicken)

Ingredients:

- 1 whole chicken
- 1 lemon
- 4 sprigs thyme
- 4 cloves garlic
- 2 tbsp butter
- 2 tbsp olive oil
- Salt and pepper to taste

An ode to simplicity and elegance—roast chicken, a classic. This dish transforms a humble bird into a masterpiece. Crispy skin, tender meat, and fragrant herbs—a symphony of flavors that encapsulates French culinary tradition.

Directions

1. Preheat oven.
2. Pat chicken dry, stuff with lemon, thyme, garlic.
3. Rub with butter, oil, seasonings.
4. Roast until golden, juices run clear.
5. Let rest, carve.
6. Serve with pan juices, revel in simplicity.

Substitutions

Any herbs for thyme, any citrus for lemon

2 servings

450 cal

45 min

Steak Frites with Béarnaise Sauce

Ingredients:

- 2 ribeye steaks
- 4 large potatoes
- 4 egg yolks
- 1 cup butter
- 2 tbsp tarragon vinegar
- 1 tbsp tarragon leaves
- Salt and pepper to taste

A celebration of indulgence—steak and fries, French style. Juicy steak, crispy fries, and velvety Béarnaise sauce. Each bite embodies the essence of French bistro dining—a perfect balance of richness and satisfaction.

Directions

1. Preheat oven, prepare fries.
2. Sear steaks in pan, finish in oven.
3. Make Béarnaise sauce with yolks, vinegar.
4. Slowly whisk in melted butter.
5. Stir in chopped tarragon, season.
6. Serve steak with fries, drizzle with sauce.
7. Savor the indulgence.

Substitutions

Any steak cut, any type of potatoes

6
servings

380 cal

3 hours

Cassoulet

A hearty embrace from the South of France—cassoulet. This stew harmonizes tender white beans, succulent meats, and savory herbs. Slow-cooked to perfection, it's a celebration of flavors that warms the soul and satisfies the senses.

Ingredients:

- 2 cups white beans
- 1 lb pork shoulder
- 1 lb sausages, 1 onion
- 2 carrots, 2 cloves garlic
- 2 cups chicken broth
- 1 cup breadcrumbs
- 2 tbsp olive oil
- 1 tsp thyme leaves
- Salt and pepper to taste

Directions

1. Soak beans, cook until tender.
2. Sauté onion, carrots, garlic.
3. Combine beans, veggies, broth.
4. Brown meats, add to pot.
5. Top with breadcrumbs, drizzle with oil.
6. Bake until golden and bubbling.
7. Sprinkle thyme, serve warm.
8. Savor each hearty spoonful.

Substitutions

Any variety of sausages

4
servings

420 cal

3 hours

Confit de Canard (Duck Confit)

Ingredients:

- 4 duck legs
- 4 cloves garlic
- 4 sprigs thyme
- 2 cups duck fat
- Salt and pepper to taste

A tender revelation—duck confit. This dish transforms duck legs into meltingly tender morsels, infused with aromatic herbs and cooked in their own rich fat. A timeless specialty that encapsulates French comfort cuisine at its finest.

Directions

1. Preheat oven.
2. Season duck legs, place in dish.
3. Add garlic, thyme, cover with duck fat.
4. Slow-cook until tender.
5. Preheat skillet, crisp skin.
6. Serve with potatoes, vegetables.
7. Indulge in the decadence.

Substitutions

Any variety of herbs for thyme

6 servings

320 cal

2.5 hours

Beef Stew (Bœuf à la Mode)

Ingredients:

- 2 lbs beef stew meat
- 2 onions, 2 carrots
- 2 cloves garlic
- 2 cups red wine
- 2 cups beef broth
- 2 tbsp tomato paste
- 2 tbsp flour
- 2 tbsp butter
- 1 tsp thyme leaves
- 1 tsp rosemary leaves, Salt and pepper to taste

A rich melody of beef and red wine—bœuf à la mode. This stew marries tender beef with a medley of vegetables and a luscious red wine sauce. Slowly simmered, it's a dish that pays homage to French culinary heritage.

Directions

1. Sauté beef in butter, remove.
2. Sauté onion, carrots, garlic.
3. Add tomato paste, flour, herbs.
4. Return beef, add wine, broth.
5. Simmer covered, then uncovered.
6. Serve with crusty bread, savor the tradition.

Substitutions

Any variety of root vegetables for carrots

4 servings

280 cal

1.5 hours

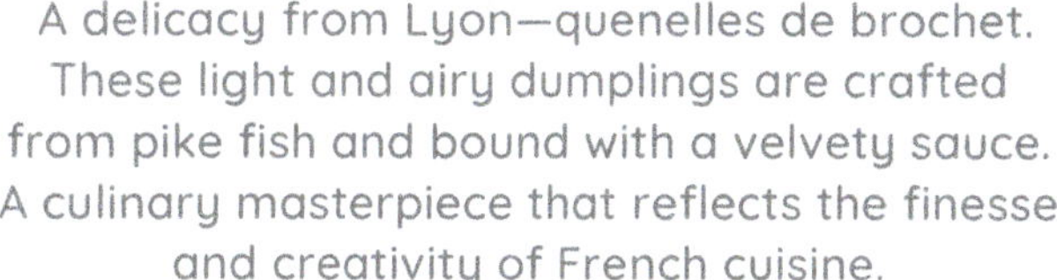

Quenelles de Brochet (Pike Dumplings)

Ingredients:

- 1 lb pike fillets
- 2 cups milk
- 1/2 cup breadcrumbs
- 2 eggs
- 1/4 tsp nutmeg
- 1/4 cup heavy cream
- 2 cups fish broth
- 2 tbsp butter
- Salt and white pepper to taste

A delicacy from Lyon—quenelles de brochet. These light and airy dumplings are crafted from pike fish and bound with a velvety sauce. A culinary masterpiece that reflects the finesse and creativity of French cuisine.

Directions

1. Purée pike fillets in food processor.
2. In saucepan, simmer milk, whisk in breadcrumbs.
3. Beat eggs, add to mixture.
4. Season with nutmeg, salt, pepper.
5. Form dumplings, poach in broth.
6. Make sauce with cream, butter, broth.
7. Serve dumplings with sauce, experience refinement.

Substitutions

Any white fish for pike, vegetable broth for fish broth

Sautéed Rabbit with Mustard

Ingredients:

- 1 rabbit (3-4 lbs)
- 2 onions
- 2 carrots
- 2 cloves garlic
- 1/4 cup Dijon mustard
- 1 cup chicken broth
- 1/2 cup white wine
- 2 tbsp olive oil
- 1 tsp thyme leaves
- Salt and pepper to taste

A rustic delight—sautéed rabbit with a touch of Dijon mustard. This dish embodies the charm of French countryside cuisine. Tender rabbit, aromatic herbs, and a hint of mustard create a symphony of flavors that transport you to a simpler time.

Directions

1. Preheat oven.
2. Cut rabbit into pieces.
3. Sauté onion, carrots, garlic.
4. Add rabbit, brown on all sides.
5. Stir in mustard, herbs.
6. Add wine, broth, simmer.
7. Finish in oven until tender.
8. Serve with crusty bread, savor the rustic charm.

Substitutions

Any white meat for rabbit, vegetable broth for chicken broth

4
servings

320 cal

1.5
hours

Chicken Fricassee

Ingredients:

- 4 chicken thighs
- 1 onion, 2 carrots
- 2 cloves garlic
- 1 cup chicken broth
- 1/2 cup white wine
- 1/2 cup heavy cream
- 2 tbsp butter
- 1 tsp tarragon leaves
- 1 tsp parsley leaves
- Salt and pepper to taste

A symphony of tender chicken and velvety sauce—chicken fricassee. This dish combines sautéed chicken with a creamy, herb-infused sauce. A culinary embrace that captures the essence of comfort and sophistication in each bite.

Directions

1. Sauté chicken until golden.
2. Sauté onion, carrots, garlic.
3. Add wine, broth, simmer.
4. Return chicken, add cream, herbs.
5. Simmer until chicken is tender.
6. Serve with rice or crusty bread, revel in comfort.

Substitutions

Any variety of herbs

4
servings

360 cal

2 hours

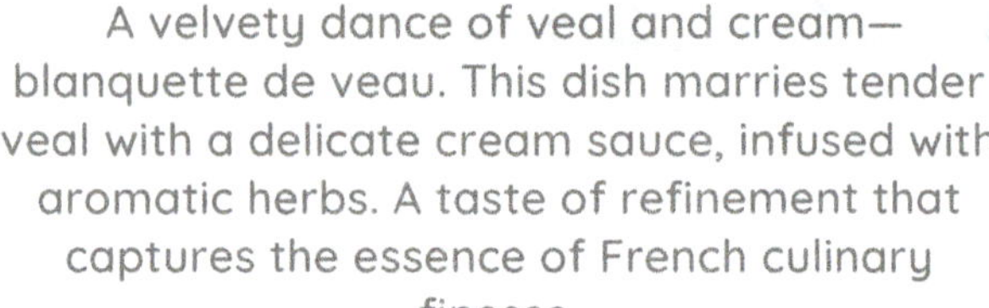

Blanquette de Veau (Veal in Cream Sauce)

Ingredients:

- 2 lbs veal stew meat
- 2 carrots
- 1 onion
- 2 cloves garlic
- 2 cups chicken broth
- 1 cup heavy cream
- 2 tbsp flour
- 2 tbsp butter
- 1 tsp thyme leaves
- 1 tsp parsley leaves
- Salt and white pepper to taste

A velvety dance of veal and cream—blanquette de veau. This dish marries tender veal with a delicate cream sauce, infused with aromatic herbs. A taste of refinement that captures the essence of French culinary finesse.

Directions

1. Sauté veal in butter until golden.
2. Sauté onion, carrots, garlic.
3. Add flour, cook briefly.
4. Add broth, simmer.
5. Return veal, add cream, herbs.
6. Simmer until veal is tender.
7. Serve with rice or crusty bread, savor the refinement.

Substitutions

Any variety of meat for veal, vegetable broth for chicken broth

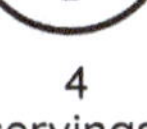

4 servings

300 cal

1.5 hours

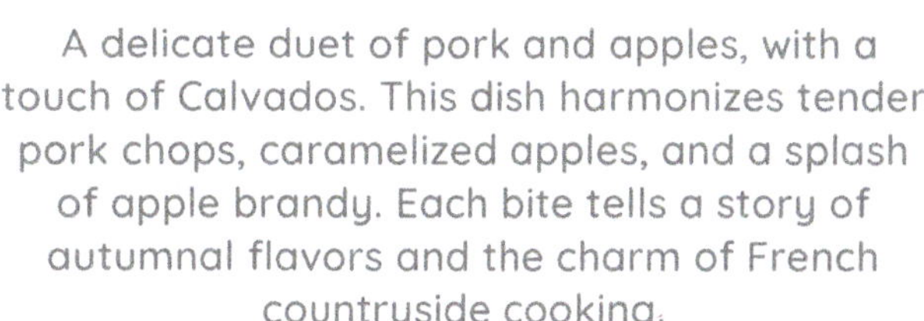

Pork Chops with Apples and Calvados

Ingredients:

- 4 pork chops
- 2 apples
- 1/4 cup Calvados (apple brandy)
- 1/2 cup chicken broth
- 1/2 cup heavy cream
- 2 tbsp butter
- 1 tsp thyme leaves
- Salt and pepper to taste

A delicate duet of pork and apples, with a touch of Calvados. This dish harmonizes tender pork chops, caramelized apples, and a splash of apple brandy. Each bite tells a story of autumnal flavors and the charm of French countryside cooking.

Directions

1. Sauté pork chops in butter.
2. Sauté apples until caramelized.
3. Deglaze pan with Calvados.
4. Add broth, cream, thyme.
5. Return pork and apples to pan.
6. Simmer until pork is cooked.
7. Serve with mashed potatoes, savor the harmony.

Substitutions

Any type of brandy for Calvados, vegetable broth for chicken broth

Chapter 4:
Homestyle Side Dishes

4
servings

150 cal

20 min

Haricots Verts Amandine (Green Beans with Almonds)

Ingredients:

- 1 lb haricots verts (French green beans)
- 1/2 cup sliced almonds
- 2 tbsp butter
- 1 lemon
- Salt and pepper to taste

A delicate dance of green beans and almonds —haricots verts amandine. This side dish marries tender beans with toasted almonds, creating a balance of textures and flavors that elevates any meal to an elegant feast.

Directions

1. Blanch beans in boiling water.
2. Sauté almonds in butter until golden.
3. Add beans, toss.
4. Squeeze lemon, season.
5. Serve warm, savor the elegance.

Substitutions

Regular green beans for haricots verts

4
servings

180 cal

40 min

Gratinéed Cauliflower

Ingredients:

- 1 head cauliflower
- 1 cup grated Gruyère cheese
- 1 cup heavy cream
- 2 tbsp breadcrumbs
- 2 tbsp butter
- 1 tsp thyme leaves
- Salt and pepper to taste

A golden symphony of comfort—gratinéed cauliflower. This dish transforms humble cauliflower into a luscious masterpiece. Baked to golden perfection with creamy sauce and melted cheese, it's a celebration of simple ingredients.

Directions

1. Preheat oven.
2. Steam cauliflower until tender.
3. Arrange cauliflower in baking dish.
4. Pour cream over cauliflower.
5. Top with cheese, breadcrumbs, thyme.
6. Dot with butter.
7. Bake until golden and bubbling.
8. Revel in the comfort.

Substitutions

Swiss cheese for Gruyère

4
servings

220 cal

40 min

Lyonnaise Potatoes

Ingredients:

- 4 large potatoes
- 1 onion
- 2 tbsp butter
- 2 tbsp olive oil
- 1 tsp thyme leaves
- Salt and pepper to taste

A rustic homage to Lyon—Lyonnaise potatoes. This side dish marries sliced potatoes with sautéed onions, creating a melody of flavors and textures that complement any main course. It's a taste of classic French bistro fare.

Directions

1. Slice potatoes, parboil briefly.
2. Sauté onion in butter and oil.
3. Add potatoes, thyme, season.
4. Sauté until golden and crispy.
5. Savor the rustic charm.

Substitutions

Any variety of herbs

6
servings

160 cal

1.5
hours

French Ratatouille

Ingredients:

- 1 eggplant
- 2 bell peppers
- 2 zucchini
- 4 tomatoes
- 1 onion
- 2 cloves garlic
- 2 tbsp olive oil
- 1 tsp thyme leaves
- 1 tsp oregano leaves
- Salt and pepper to taste

A vibrant ode to Provence—French ratatouille. This vegetable medley dances with colors, textures, and flavors. Layers of eggplant, peppers, zucchini, and tomatoes slowly simmer to create a dish that captures the essence of southern France.

Directions

1. Slice vegetables, sauté onion, garlic.
2. Layer veggies in dish, drizzle oil.
3. Season with herbs, salt, pepper.
4. Cover, simmer until tender.
5. Serve warm, savor the sunshine.

Substitutions

Any variety of vegetables

4
servings

220 cal

1.5
hours

Spinach Soufflé

Ingredients:

- 2 cups cooked spinach
- 4 eggs
- 1 cup milk
- 1/2 cup grated Parmesan cheese
- 2 tbsp butter
- 2 tbsp flour
- Nutmeg to taste
- Salt and pepper to taste

A delicate rise of flavors—spinach soufflé. This dish blends tender spinach with a fluffy soufflé base, creating an airy creation that melts in your mouth. Each bite is a celebration of the artistry and elegance of French cooking.

Directions

1. Preheat oven.
2. Sauté spinach in butter.
3. Make roux with butter and flour.
4. Add milk, seasonings, cook until thick.
5. Stir in spinach and cheese.
6. Separate egg yolks, whisk into mixture.
7. Beat egg whites, fold into mixture.
8. Bake until puffed and golden.
9. Revel in the elegance.

Substitutions

Any variety of greens for spinach

4
servings

120 cal

30 min

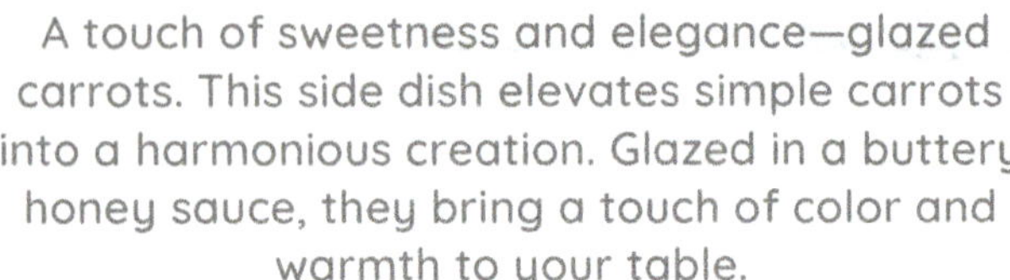

Glazed Carrots

Ingredients:

- 1 lb baby carrots
- 2 tbsp butter
- 2 tbsp honey
- 1 tsp thyme leaves
- Salt and pepper to taste

A touch of sweetness and elegance—glazed carrots. This side dish elevates simple carrots into a harmonious creation. Glazed in a buttery honey sauce, they bring a touch of color and warmth to your table.

Directions

1. Sauté carrots in butter.
2. Add honey, thyme, seasonings.
3. Sauté until glazed and tender.
4. Serve warm, savor the sweetness.

Substitutions

Any variety of herbs

4
servings

280 cal

1.5
hours

Pommes Anna (Layered Potatoes)

Ingredients:

- 4 large potatoes
- 1/2 cup butter
- Salt and pepper to taste

A symphony of layers and textures—Pommes Anna. This dish transforms potatoes into a tower of golden elegance. Thinly sliced and layered with butter, each bite is a balance of crispy edges and tender insides. A tribute to classic French technique.

Directions

1. Preheat oven.
2. Slice potatoes thinly.
3. Melt butter.
4. Layer potatoes, brush with butter.
5. Repeat layers, season.
6. Bake until golden and crispy.
7. Revel in the artistry.

Substitutions

Any variety of herbs

4 servings

180 cal

40 min

Fennel Gratin

Ingredients:

- 2 fennel bulbs
- 1 cup grated Gruyère cheese
- 1 cup heavy cream
- 2 tbsp breadcrumbs
- 2 tbsp butter
- 1 tsp thyme leaves
- Salt and pepper to taste

A celebration of flavors and layers—fennel gratin. This side dish marries tender fennel with a velvety sauce and melted cheese. Baked to golden perfection, it's a taste of refinement that adds elegance to any meal.

Directions

1. Preheat oven.
2. Slice fennel bulbs.
3. Steam fennel until tender.
4. Arrange fennel in baking dish.
5. Pour cream over fennel.
6. Top with cheese, breadcrumbs, thyme.
7. Dot with butter.
8. Bake until golden and bubbling.
9. Savor the refinement.

Substitutions

Swiss cheese for Gruyère

4 servings

160 cal

1 hour

Roasted Root Vegetables

Ingredients:

- 2 carrots
- 2 parsnips
- 2 beets
- 2 potatoes
- 2 tbsp olive oil
- 1 tsp thyme leaves
- 1 tsp rosemary leaves
- Salt and pepper to taste

A celebration of earthy flavors and textures—roasted root vegetables. This side dish brings together a medley of root vegetables, roasted to caramelized perfection. A rustic homage to nature's bounty, it's a taste of comfort and warmth.

Directions

1. Preheat oven.
2. Peel and chop vegetables.
3. Toss with olive oil, herbs, seasonings.
4. Roast until caramelized and tender.
5. Savor the rustic goodness.

Substitutions

Any variety of root vegetables

4
servings

150 cal

30 min

Mushroom Duxelles

Ingredients:

- 1 lb mushrooms
- 1 shallot
- 2 cloves garlic
- 2 tbsp butter
- 2 tbsp olive oil
- 1 tsp thyme leaves
- Salt and pepper to taste

An umami-rich delight—mushroom duxelles. This side dish blends finely chopped mushrooms with aromatic herbs, creating a paste that adds depth to dishes. A versatile creation that embodies the heart of French culinary technique.

Directions

1. Finely chop mushrooms, shallot, garlic.
2. Sauté mixture in butter and oil.
3. Add thyme, seasonings.
4. Cook until mixture is dry and paste-like.
5. Use as a base, spread, or flavor enhancer.
6. Revel in the umami.

Substitutions

Any variety of mushrooms

Chapter 5:
Decadent Desserts

4
servings

320 cal

2 hours

Crème Brûlée

Ingredients:

- 2 cups heavy cream
- 4 egg yolks
- 1/2 cup granulated sugar
- 1 tsp vanilla extract
- 4 tsp brown sugar

A delicate balance of creaminess and crackling—crème brûlée. This dessert marries velvety custard with a crisp caramelized sugar crust. Each spoonful is a dance of textures and flavors that embody French dessert elegance.

Directions

1. Preheat oven.
2. Heat cream until warm.
3. Whisk yolks, sugar, vanilla.
4. Gradually add cream, strain.
5. Divide into ramekins, bake in water bath.
6. Chill until set.
7. Sprinkle brown sugar, caramelize with torch.
8. Savor the creamy crunch.

Substitutions

Any flavoring for vanilla

6
servings

280 cal

1.5
hours

Tarte Tatin

Ingredients:

- 6 apples
- 1 cup granulated sugar
- 1/2 cup butter
- 1 tsp vanilla extract
- 1 sheet puff pastry

A caramelized masterpiece—Tarte Tatin. This upside-down caramelized apple tart is a blend of golden sweetness and flaky pastry. With each slice, you're experiencing a taste of French patisserie at its finest.

Directions

1. Preheat oven.
2. Caramelize sugar in butter.
3. Add apples, vanilla, cook until caramelized.
4. Roll out puff pastry, cover apples.
5. Bake until golden.
6. Invert onto plate, savor the indulgence.

Substitutions

Any type of fruit for apples

4 servings   **250 cal**   **2 hours**

Chocolate Mousse

Ingredients:

- 6 oz semi-sweet chocolate
- 1 cup heavy cream
- 4 egg yolks
- 1/4 cup granulated sugar
- 1 tsp vanilla extract
- Pinch of salt

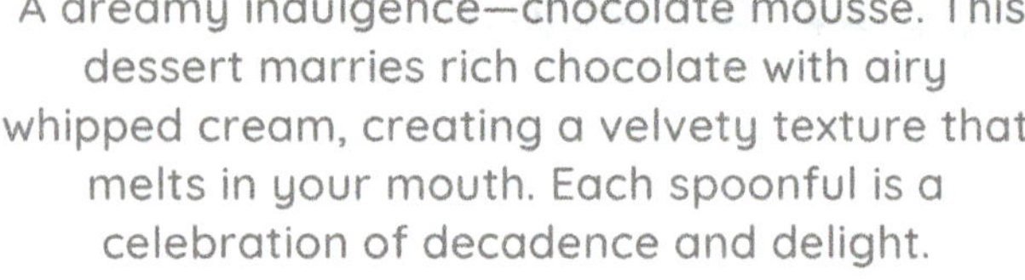

A dreamy indulgence—chocolate mousse. This dessert marries rich chocolate with airy whipped cream, creating a velvety texture that melts in your mouth. Each spoonful is a celebration of decadence and delight.

Directions

1. Melt chocolate, let cool.
2. Whip cream until soft peaks form.
3. Beat yolks, sugar, vanilla, salt.
4. Fold yolks into chocolate.
5. Gently fold in whipped cream.
6. Divide into serving dishes, chill until set.
7. Savor the lusciousness.

Substitutions

Any type of chocolate

4
servings

320 cal

2 hours

Profiteroles with Vanilla Ice Cream and Chocolate Sauce

Ingredients:

- 1/2 cup water
- 1/4 cup butter
- 1/2 cup all-purpose flour
- 2 eggs
- 1 pint vanilla ice cream
- 1/2 cup chocolate chips
- 1/4 cup heavy cream

An indulgent trio—profiteroles with ice cream and chocolate. These delicate pastry puffs are filled with creamy vanilla ice cream and drizzled with luscious chocolate sauce. A dessert that brings together textures and flavors in perfect harmony.

Directions

1. Preheat oven.
2. Boil water, butter.
3. Stir in flour, cook until dough forms.
4. Beat in eggs, pipe onto baking sheet.
5. Bake until golden.
6. Warm chocolate and cream, make sauce.
7. Split profiteroles, fill with ice cream.
8. Drizzle with chocolate sauce.
9. Savor the trio of delights.

Substitutions

Any flavor of ice cream, any type of chocolate

24
cookies

80 cal
per
cookie

1.5
hours

Madeleines

Ingredients:

- 2/3 cup all-purpose flour
- 1/2 cup granulated sugar
- 2 eggs
- 1/2 cup butter (melted)
- 1 tsp baking powder
- 1 tsp vanilla extract
- 1 lemon (zest)

A journey through flavor and nostalgia—madeleines. These delicate shell-shaped cakes are infused with lemon zest, creating a subtle citrus aroma and tender crumb. With each bite, you're transported to the heart of French pastry tradition.

Directions

1. Preheat oven.
2. Beat eggs, sugar until pale.
3. Add vanilla, lemon zest, butter.
4. Fold in flour, baking powder.
5. Chill batter, spoon into molds.
6. Bake until golden and springy.
7. Savor the nostalgic delight.

Substitutions

Any citrus zest for lemon

6
servings

210 cal

1.5
hours

Clafoutis

Ingredients:

- 2 cups pitted cherries
- 1/2 cup all-purpose flour
- 1/2 cup granulated sugar
- 3 eggs
- 1 cup milk
- 1 tsp vanilla extract
- Pinch of salt

A celebration of fruits and custard—clafoutis. This dessert harmonizes tender fruit with a custard-like batter, creating a textured delight that's as rustic as it is elegant. With each bite, you're experiencing a taste of French countryside comfort.

Directions

1. Preheat oven.
2. Arrange cherries in baking dish.
3. Whisk flour, sugar, eggs, milk, vanilla, salt.
4. Pour batter over cherries.
5. Bake until golden and set.
6. Revel in the rustic elegance.

Substitutions

Any variety of fruit for cherries

4 servings **280 cal** **1.5 hours**

Crêpes Suzette

Ingredients:

- 1 cup all-purpose flour
- 2/3 cup milk
- 2 eggs
- 1/4 cup orange juice
- 1/4 cup orange liqueur
- 1/4 cup granulated sugar
- 2 tbsp butter
- 1 orange (zest)
- 2 oranges (segments)

A flambéed romance of crêpes—Crêpes Suzette. These delicate pancakes are bathed in a luscious orange sauce, then flambéed to perfection. Each bite is a taste of elegance and showmanship that captures the heart of French dessert theatre.

Directions

1. Whisk flour, milk, eggs until smooth.
2. Heat pan, make crêpes.
3. Make syrup with orange juice, sugar, zest.
4. Fold crêpes, warm in syrup.
5. Add orange liqueur, flambé.
6. Serve with orange segments.
7. Revel in the theatrics.

Substitutions

Any type of liqueur

6 servings   **280 cal**   **2 hours**

Éclair au Chocolat

Ingredients:

- 1/2 cup water
- 1/4 cup butter
- 1/2 cup all-purpose flour
- 2 eggs
- 1 cup milk
- 1/4 cup granulated sugar
- 2 tbsp cocoa powder
- 2 oz dark chocolate

A choux pastry masterpiece—Éclair au Chocolat. These delicate pastries are filled with creamy chocolate custard and glazed with glossy chocolate. Each bite is a harmonious blend of textures and flavors that embodies French patisserie elegance.

Directions

1. Preheat oven.
2. Boil water, butter.
3. Stir in flour, cook until dough forms.
4. Beat in eggs, pipe onto baking sheet.
5. Bake until golden.
6. Heat milk, sugar, cocoa.
7. Beat in egg, cook until thick.
8. Fill éclairs with custard.
9. Melt chocolate, glaze éclairs.
10. Revel in the decadence.

Substitutions

Any type of chocolate

4
servings

180 cal

1.5
hours

Floating Island (Île Flottante)

Ingredients:

- 4 egg whites
- 1 cup milk
- 1/4 cup granulated sugar
- 1 tsp vanilla extract
- 1/4 cup caramel sauce

A delicate dance of poached meringue and custard—Île Flottante. This dessert features soft meringue floating on a sea of creamy custard. Each bite is a balance of textures and flavors that embodies the finesse of French dessert craftsmanship.

Directions

1. Beat egg whites until stiff peaks form.
2. Poach spoonfuls in milk until set.
3. Heat milk, sugar, vanilla for custard.
4. Pour custard into serving dishes.
5. Place meringue on custard, drizzle with caramel.
6. Savor the delicate delight.

Substitutions

Any type of sauce for caramel

6 servings
260 cal
1.5 hours

Apple Galette

Ingredients:

- 1 sheet puff pastry
- 4 apples
- 1/4 cup granulated sugar
- 1 tsp cinnamon
- 1 egg (for egg wash)

A rustic celebration of apples—apple galette. This free-form tart marries thinly sliced apples with flaky pastry, creating a dish that captures the heart of French countryside baking. With each bite, you're experiencing the comfort and simplicity of nature's bounty.

Directions

1. Preheat oven.
2. Roll out puff pastry.
3. Arrange apple slices, leaving a border.
4. Sprinkle sugar, cinnamon over apples.
5. Fold edges of pastry over apples.
6. Brush pastry with egg wash.
7. Bake until golden and fragrant.
8. Revel in the rustic charm.

Substitutions

Any variety of fruit for apples

Your support would mean the world to us.

Reviews are hard to come by, and if you can take a moment, we'd greatly appreciate your support. Please go back to your app or where you made your purchase, click on the review button, and give us a rating along with a short sentence. We truly value your feedback. Being a small publisher, reviews are hard to come by, and a review from you could help us drastically. Rest assured, we read and appreciate every single review. Now, let's get back to the delicious recipes!

Chapter 6:
Rustic Breads and Pastries

1
baguett
e

220 cal

4 hours

Baguette

Ingredients:

- 3 cups bread flour
- 2 tsp salt
- 1 1/4 cups warm water
- 2 tsp active dry yeast

A quintessential French classic—baguette. This long, slender loaf boasts a crisp crust and tender interior. With each slice, you're transported to a Parisian bakery, savoring the simplicity and beauty of French bread craftsmanship.

Directions

1. Mix flour, yeast, salt.
2. Add water, knead to form dough.
3. Let rise until doubled.
4. Shape into baguette, let rise again.
5. Preheat oven, slash top of baguette.
6. Bake until golden and crusty.
7. Savor the Parisian delight.

Substitutions

Any type of flour

1 loaf   250 cal   5 hours

Pain de Campagne (Country Bread)

Ingredients:

- 2 cups bread flour
- 1 cup whole wheat flour
- 1 cup rye flour
- 2 tsp salt
- 1 1/4 cups warm water
- 2 tsp active dry yeast

A rustic symphony of grains—Pain de Campagne. This hearty country bread marries a mix of flours, creating a flavorful and textured loaf. Each slice embodies the warmth and simplicity of French countryside baking.

Directions

1. Mix flours, yeast, salt.
2. Add water, knead to form dough.
3. Let rise until doubled.
4. Shape into loaf, let rise again.
5. Preheat oven, slash top of loaf.
6. Bake until golden and hearty.
7. Revel in the rustic charm.

Substitutions

Any type of flour

1 loaf   **240 cal**   **5 hours**

Pain Complet (Whole Wheat Bread)

Ingredients:

- 3 cups whole wheat flour
- 2 tsp salt
- 1 1/4 cups warm water
- 2 tsp active dry yeast

A wholesome embrace of whole grains—Pain Complet. This hearty whole wheat bread is a celebration of natural flavors and textures. With each slice, you're savoring the richness and goodness of whole wheat goodness.

Directions

1. Mix flour, yeast, salt.
2. Add water, knead to form dough.
3. Let rise until doubled.
4. Shape into loaf, let rise again.
5. Preheat oven, slash top of loaf.
6. Bake until golden and hearty.
7. Savor the wholesome delight.

Substitutions

Any type of flour

1
fougasse

280 cal

4 hours

Fougasse with Herbs and Olives

Ingredients:

- 3 cups bread flour
- 2 tsp salt
- 1 1/4 cups warm water
- 2 tsp active dry yeast
- 1/4 cup olive oil
- 1/2 cup mixed fresh herbs (rosemary, thyme, oregano)
- 1/2 cup Kalamata olives (pitted and chopped)

A work of art in bread—Fougasse with herbs and olives. This decorative flatbread is shaped like a leaf or an ear of wheat, and it's adorned with fragrant herbs and savory olives. A testament to the creativity and flavor of French baking.

Directions

1. Mix flour, yeast, salt.
2. Add water, knead to form dough.
3. Let rise until doubled.
4. Roll out dough, shape fougasse.
5. Press in herbs and olives.
6. Let rise again.
7. Preheat oven, bake until golden.
8. Savor the artistic creation.

Substitutions

Any type of fresh herbs, any type of olives

12 croissants

180 cal per croissant

8 hours

Croissants

A flaky marvel of French pastry—croissants. These buttery crescent-shaped pastries are a blend of tender layers and rich flavor. With each bite, you're experiencing the elegance and indulgence of French breakfast tradition.

Ingredients:

- 3 1/2 cups bread flour
- 1/4 cup granulated sugar
- 1 tsp salt
- 1 1/4 cups warm milk
- 2 tsp active dry yeast
- 1/2 cup unsalted butter (cold)
- 1 cup unsalted butter (softened)
- 1 egg (for egg wash)

Directions

1. Mix flour, sugar, salt.
2. Add milk, yeast, knead dough.
3. Let rise until doubled.
4. Roll out dough, dot with cold butter.
5. Fold, chill, repeat folding.
6. Roll out dough, cut into triangles.
7. Shape croissants, let rise.
8. Brush with egg wash, bake until golden.
9. Revel in the flakiness.

Substitutions

Any type of butter

1 loaf   260 cal   5 hours

Pain aux Raisins (Raisin Bread)

Ingredients:

- 3 cups bread flour
- 1/4 cup granulated sugar
- 2 tsp salt
- 1 1/4 cups warm water
- 2 tsp active dry yeast
- 1/2 cup raisins
- 1/4 cup pastry cream

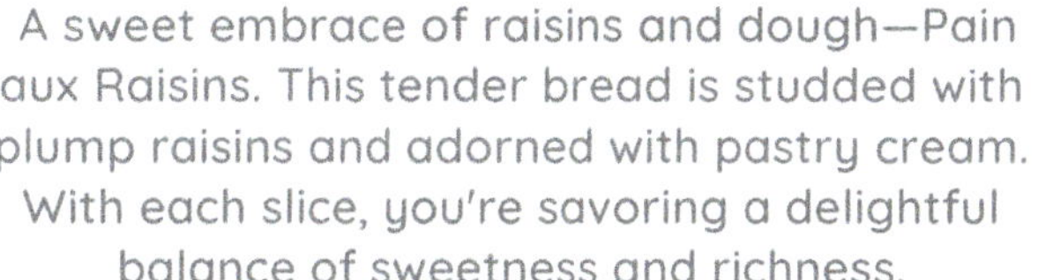

A sweet embrace of raisins and dough—Pain aux Raisins. This tender bread is studded with plump raisins and adorned with pastry cream. With each slice, you're savoring a delightful balance of sweetness and richness.

Directions

1. Mix flour, sugar, salt.
2. Add water, yeast, knead dough.
3. Let rise until doubled.
4. Knead in raisins, shape loaf.
5. Let rise again.
6. Preheat oven, bake until golden.
7. Fill center with pastry cream.
8. Savor the sweet richness.

Substitutions

Any type of dried fruit for raisins

4
servings

280 cal

30 min

Pain Perdu (French Toast)

Ingredients:

- 8 slices stale bread
- 2 eggs
- 1/2 cup milk
- 1/4 cup granulated sugar
- 1 tsp vanilla extract, Butter (for cooking),
- Maple syrup (for serving)

A delicious resurrection of bread—Pain Perdu. This classic dish takes stale bread and transforms it into a breakfast masterpiece. With each bite, you're experiencing a comforting embrace of flavors and textures.

Directions

1. Beat eggs, milk, sugar, vanilla.
2. Dip bread slices in mixture.
3. Heat butter in pan.
4. Cook bread until golden.
5. Serve with maple syrup.
6. Savor the breakfast resurrection.

Substitutions

Any type of syrup

1 loaf   300 cal   6 hours

Brioche

Ingredients:

- 3 1/2 cups bread flour
- 1/4 cup granulated sugar
- 1 tsp salt
- 1 1/4 cups warm milk
- 2 tsp active dry yeast
- 3 eggs
- 1/2 cup unsalted butter (softened)

A buttery delight in bread—Brioche. This rich and tender bread boasts a golden crust and soft interior. With each slice, you're savoring the elegance and indulgence of French baking, whether enjoyed plain or as the base for other culinary delights.

Directions

1. Mix flour, sugar, salt.
2. Add milk, yeast, knead dough.
3. Let rise until doubled.
4. Beat eggs, add to dough.
5. Knead in softened butter.
6. Let rise again.
7. Shape into loaf, let rise.
8. Preheat oven, bake until golden.
9. Revel in the buttery goodness.

Substitutions

Any type of butter

6 servings **240 cal** **2 hours**

Pissaladière (Onion and Anchovy Tart)

Ingredients:

- 1 sheet puff pastry
- 4 cups yellow onions (sliced)
- 1/4 cup olive oil
- 12 anchovy fillets
- 1/2 cup Niçoise olives (pitted)
- 1 tsp thyme leaves

A savory masterpiece of onions and anchovies —Pissaladière. This tart showcases the bold flavors of the Mediterranean, with caramelized onions, salty anchovies, and olives. With each bite, you're transported to the sun-soaked shores of Provence.

Directions

1. Preheat oven.
2. Sauté onions in olive oil until caramelized.
3. Roll out puff pastry, transfer to baking sheet.
4. Spread onions over pastry.
5. Arrange anchovies, olives, thyme.
6. Bake until golden and fragrant.
7. Savor the Mediterranean flavors.

Substitutions

Any type of olives

24 puffs

60 cal per puff

1.5 hours

Gougères (Cheese Puffs)

Ingredients:

- 1/2 cup water
- 1/4 cup unsalted butter
- 1/2 cup all-purpose flour
- 2 eggs
- 1/2 cup grated Gruyère cheese
- 1/2 tsp salt
- 1/4 tsp black pepper
- Pinch of nutmeg

A cheesy delight in puff form—Gougères. These savory puffs are a blend of choux pastry and grated cheese, creating a light and flavorful bite-sized treat. With each puff, you're experiencing the joy and simplicity of French baking.

Directions

1. Preheat oven.
2. Boil water, butter.
3. Stir in flour, cook until dough forms.
4. Beat in eggs, add cheese, seasonings.
5. Pipe onto baking sheet.
6. Bake until puffed and golden.
7. Savor the cheesy goodness.

Substitutions

Any type of cheese

Chapter 7:
Cozy Breakfast and Brunch

1
omelette

220 cal

15 min

Omelette aux Fines Herbes

Ingredients:

- 3 eggs
- 2 tbsp mixed fresh herbs (parsley, chives, tarragon)
- Salt and pepper to taste
- Butter (for cooking)

A harmonious dance of eggs and herbs—Omelette aux Fines Herbes. This classic French omelette showcases the elegance of simplicity, with a delicate blend of fresh herbs. With each bite, you're experiencing the art of French egg cookery.

Directions

1. Beat eggs, herbs, salt, and pepper.
2. Heat butter in pan.
3. Pour in eggs, cook gently.
4. Fold and shape omelette.
5. Savor the herbaceous delight.

Substitutions

Any type of fresh herbs

2
sandwic
hes

350 cal
per
sandwic
h

25 min

Croque-Monsieur

Ingredients:

- 4 slices sandwich bread
- 4 slices ham
- 1 1/2 cups Gruyère cheese (grated)
- 2 cups béchamel sauce
- Dijon mustard (optional)
- Butter (for cooking)

An indulgent twist on a sandwich—Croque-Monsieur. This grilled ham and cheese sandwich is elevated with creamy béchamel and a crispy crust. With each bite, you're experiencing the rich comfort of French café cuisine.

Directions

1. Preheat oven.
2. Spread mustard on bread slices (optional).
3. Layer ham and cheese between slices.
4. Pour béchamel over sandwiches.
5. Grill until golden and bubbling.
6. Savor the melty indulgence.

Substitutions

Any type of cheese

1 quiche   280 cal   1.5 hours

Quiche aux Asperges (Asparagus Quiche)

Ingredients:

- 1 pie crust
- 1 1/2 cups asparagus (trimmed and blanched)
- 1 cup Gruyère cheese (grated)
- 4 eggs
- 1 cup heavy cream
- 1/2 tsp nutmeg
- Salt and pepper to taste

Substitutions

Any type of cheese

A slice of spring in a quiche—Quiche aux Asperges. This savory tart features tender asparagus and creamy custard in a flaky crust. With each bite, you're savoring the freshness and elegance of French quiche tradition.

Directions

1. Preheat oven.
2. Arrange asparagus on pie crust.
3. Sprinkle with cheese.
4. Beat eggs, cream, nutmeg, salt, and pepper.
5. Pour custard over asparagus.
6. Bake until set and golden.
7. Savor the taste of spring.

4
servings

300 cal

30 min

Pain Perdu with Berries

Ingredients:

- 8 slices stale bread
- 2 eggs
- 1/2 cup milk
- 1/4 cup granulated sugar
- 1 tsp vanilla extract
- Butter (for cooking)
- Fresh berries (strawberries, blueberries, raspberries)

A berry-filled twist on a classic—Pain Perdu with Berries. This French toast is adorned with fresh berries, creating a burst of color and flavor. With each bite, you're experiencing the perfect marriage of sweetness and comfort.

Directions

1. Beat eggs, milk, sugar, vanilla.
2. Dip bread slices in mixture.
3. Heat butter in pan.
4. Cook bread until golden.
5. Top with fresh berries.
6. Savor the berry delight.

Substitutions

Any type of berries

4
servings

260 cal

30 min

Crêpes with Ham and Cheese

Ingredients:

- 1 cup all-purpose flour
- 2 eggs
- 1 1/4 cups milk
- 2 tbsp butter (melted)
- 1/2 cup grated Gruyère cheese
- 1/2 cup cooked ham (diced)
- Salt and pepper to taste

A savory delight in thin form—Crêpes with Ham and Cheese. These delicate pancakes are filled with ham and melted cheese, creating a savory sensation. With each bite, you're savoring the harmonious blend of textures and flavors.

Directions

1. Blend flour, eggs, milk, and butter.
2. Heat pan, make crêpes.
3. Fill crêpes with ham and cheese.
4. Fold and warm until cheese melts.
5. Savor the savory delight.

Substitutions

Any type of cheese, any type of cooked meat

4 servings

320 cal

45 min

Rösti with Smoked Salmon

Ingredients:

- 4 large potatoes
- 1/4 cup butter
- Salt and pepper to taste
- 4 oz smoked salmon
- Sour cream and chives (for serving)

A Swiss-inspired delight with French flair—Rösti with Smoked Salmon. This potato pancake is adorned with luscious smoked salmon, creating a luxurious breakfast treat. With each bite, you're experiencing a taste of Alpine comfort and elegance.

Directions

1. Peel and grate potatoes.
2. Squeeze out excess moisture.
3. Season with salt and pepper.
4. Heat butter in pan.
5. Press potatoes into pan, cook until golden.
6. Flip and cook the other side.
7. Top with smoked salmon.
8. Serve with sour cream and chives.
9. Revel in the luxurious simplicity.

Substitutions

Any type of smoked fish

4 servings

220 cal

15 min

Yogurt Parfait with Granola and Berries

Ingredients:

- 2 cups Greek yogurt
- 1 cup granola
- 1 cup mixed berries (strawberries, blueberries, raspberries)
- Honey (for drizzling)

A layered delight of freshness—Yogurt Parfait with Granola and Berries. This parfait combines creamy yogurt, crunchy granola, and vibrant berries. With each spoonful, you're savoring a balanced and refreshing start to the day.

Directions

1. Layer yogurt, granola, and berries in glasses.
2. Drizzle with honey.
3. Savor the refreshing layers.

Substitutions

Any type of granola, any type of berries

6 servings

290 cal

1.5 hours

French Toast Casserole

Ingredients:

- 8 slices stale bread
- 6 eggs
- 2 cups milk
- 1/4 cup granulated sugar
- 1 tsp vanilla extract
- Cinnamon and nutmeg to taste
- Butter (for greasing)

A comforting embrace in casserole form—French Toast Casserole. This baked dish features bread soaked in custard, creating a rich and satisfying breakfast. With each spoonful, you're experiencing the warmth and heartiness of French comfort food.

Directions

1. Grease baking dish with butter.
2. Arrange bread slices in dish.
3. Beat eggs, milk, sugar, vanilla, spices.
4. Pour custard over bread.
5. Let soak, press bread down.
6. Preheat oven, bake until set.
7. Savor the comforting casserole.

Substitutions

Any type of spices

4
galettes

280 cal
per
galette

1 hour

Buckwheat Galettes with Egg and Cheese

Ingredients:

- 1 cup buckwheat flour
- 2 eggs
- 1 1/4 cups water
- Salt to taste
- Butter (for cooking)
- 4 eggs
- 1 cup grated Gruyère cheese

A savory delight with a rustic charm—Buckwheat Galettes with Egg and Cheese. These earthy buckwheat crepes are filled with egg and cheese, creating a satisfying and flavorful meal. With each bite, you're transported to the rustic heart of French countryside cooking.

Directions

1. Mix buckwheat flour, eggs, water, salt.
2. Heat pan, make galettes.
3. Cook eggs in separate pan.
4. Fill galettes with egg and cheese.
5. Fold and warm until cheese melts.
6. Revel in the rustic goodness.

Substitutions

Any type of cheese

4
servings

240 cal

45 min

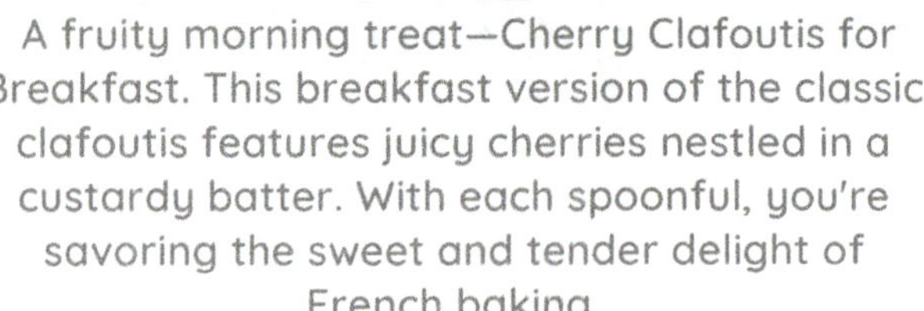

Cherry Clafoutis for Breakfast

Ingredients:

- 2 cups fresh cherries (pitted)
- 1/4 cup granulated sugar
- 1/2 cup all-purpose flour
- 3 eggs
- 1 cup milk
- 1 tsp vanilla extract
- Powdered sugar (for dusting)

A fruity morning treat—Cherry Clafoutis for Breakfast. This breakfast version of the classic clafoutis features juicy cherries nestled in a custardy batter. With each spoonful, you're savoring the sweet and tender delight of French baking.

Directions

1. Preheat oven.
2. Arrange cherries in baking dish.
3. Sprinkle with sugar.
4. Blend flour, eggs, milk, vanilla.
5. Pour batter over cherries.
6. Bake until golden and set.
7. Dust with powdered sugar.
8. Savor the fruity delight.

Substitutions

Any type of fruit for cherries

Chapter 8:
Family-Favorite
Poultry Dishes

6 servings **380 cal** **2 hours**

Chicken Pot Pie

Ingredients:

- 1 pie crust
- 2 cups cooked chicken (shredded)
- 1 cup mixed vegetables (peas, carrots, corn)
- 1/4 cup butter
- 1/4 cup all-purpose flour
- 2 cups chicken broth
- 1/2 cup milk
- Salt and pepper to taste
- Thyme leaves (optional)

A timeless comfort in pie form—Chicken Pot Pie. This dish is a medley of tender chicken, hearty vegetables, and creamy sauce, all encased in a flaky crust. With each bite, you're experiencing the warmth and familiarity of family cooking.

Directions

1. Preheat oven.
2. Melt butter, sauté vegetables.
3. Stir in flour, cook until bubbly.
4. Add broth, milk, seasonings.
5. Simmer until thickened.
6. Stir in chicken and thyme.
7. Pour filling into pie crust.
8. Top with another pie crust.
9. Bake until golden and bubbling.
10. Savor the comforting pie.

Substitutions

Any type of cooked meat, any type of vegetables

4
servings

320 cal

45 min

Chicken à la Normande

Ingredients:

- 4 chicken breasts (boneless and skinless)
- 2 apples (peeled, cored, and sliced)
- 1/2 cup apple brandy (Calvados)
v1/2 cup heavy cream
- 1/4 cup chicken broth
v2 tbsp butter
- Salt and pepper to taste
- Fresh parsley (for garnish)

An elegant French countryside dish—Chicken à la Normande. This dish combines tender chicken with apples and cream, creating a harmonious blend of flavors. With each bite, you're savoring the balance of richness and sweetness.

Directions

1. Season chicken with salt and pepper.
2. Heat butter, brown chicken.
3. Remove chicken from pan.
4. Sauté apples in the same pan.
5. Deglaze with apple brandy.
6. Add cream and broth, simmer.
7. Return chicken to pan, cook until done.
8. Garnish with parsley.
9. Savor the elegant flavors.

Substitutions

Any type of brandy

4
servings

340 cal

1.5
hours

Chicken and Mushroom Vol-au-Vent

Ingredients:

- 1 sheet puff pastry
- 2 cups cooked chicken (cubed)
- 1 cup mushrooms (sliced)
- 1/4 cup butter
- 1/4 cup all-purpose flour
- 1 1/2 cups chicken broth
v1/2 cup heavy cream
- Salt and pepper to taste
vFresh thyme leaves

Substitutions

Any type of cooked meat, any type of mushrooms

A puff pastry delight—Chicken and Mushroom Vol-au-Vent. This dish features a creamy chicken and mushroom filling nestled in delicate puff pastry. With each bite, you're experiencing the decadence and charm of French pastry.

Directions

1. Preheat oven.
2. Roll out and cut puff pastry.
3. Bake until golden.
4. Melt butter, sauté mushrooms.
5. Stir in flour, cook until bubbly.
6. Add broth, cream, seasonings.
7. Simmer until thickened.
8. Stir in chicken and thyme.
9. Warm pastry shells.
10. Fill with chicken and mushroom mixture.
11. Savor the pastry perfection.

4
servings

300 cal

1.5
hours

Chicken Fricassée with Tarragon

Ingredients:

- 4 chicken thighs (bone-in and skin-on)
- 1/2 cup all-purpose flour
- 1/4 cup butter
- 1 cup chicken broth
- 1/2 cup white wine
- 1/4 cup heavy cream
- 2 tbsp fresh tarragon leaves
- Salt and pepper to taste

A fragrant embrace of herbs—Chicken Fricassée with Tarragon. This dish features tender chicken in a creamy tarragon sauce. With each bite, you're savoring the aromatic richness of French herb-infused cuisine.

Directions

1. Season chicken with salt and pepper.
2. Dredge in flour, shake off excess.
3. Heat butter, brown chicken.
4. Remove chicken from pan.
5. Deglaze with wine, reduce.
6. Add broth, simmer.
7. Return chicken to pan, cook until done.
8. Stir in cream and tarragon.
9. Savor the fragrant flavors.

Substitutions

Any type of herbs

8 servings

180 cal per serving

1 hour

Chicken Liver Pâté with Cornichons

Ingredients:

- 1/2 lb chicken livers
- 1/2 cup onions (chopped)
- 1/4 cup butter
- 2 cloves garlic (minced)
- 1/4 cup brandy
- 1/4 cup heavy cream
- Salt and pepper to taste
- Fresh thyme leaves (for garnish)
- Cornichons (for serving)

An indulgent spread with tangy flair—Chicken Liver Pâté with Cornichons. This pâté is a blend of rich chicken liver and zesty cornichons, creating a delightful appetizer. With each bite, you're experiencing the balance of flavors and textures.

Directions

1. Sauté onions in butter.
2. Add garlic, livers, cook until done.
3. Deglaze with brandy, reduce.
4. Purée mixture in food processor.
5. Add cream, seasonings, blend until smooth.
6. Transfer to serving dish, garnish with thyme.
7. Serve with cornichons.
8. Savor the indulgence.

Substitutions

Any type of brandy

4 servings

380 cal

1.5 hours

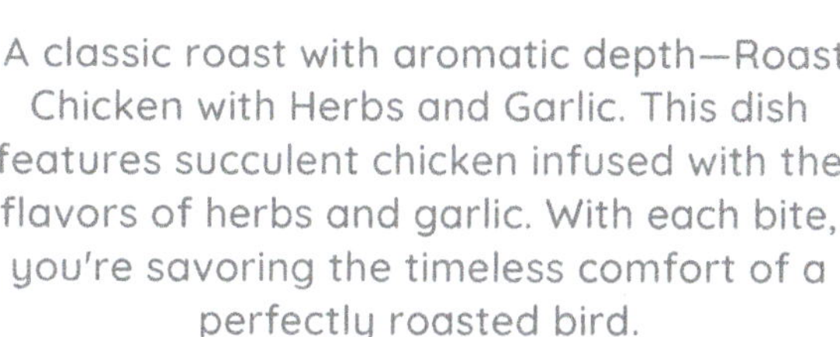

Roast Chicken with Herbs and Garlic

Ingredients:

- 1 whole chicken (about 4 lbs)
- 1/4 cup butter (softened)
- 4 cloves garlic (minced)
- 2 tbsp mixed fresh herbs (rosemary, thyme, parsley)
- Salt and pepper to taste
- Lemon wedges (for serving)

A classic roast with aromatic depth—Roast Chicken with Herbs and Garlic. This dish features succulent chicken infused with the flavors of herbs and garlic. With each bite, you're savoring the timeless comfort of a perfectly roasted bird.

Directions

1. Preheat oven.
2. Mix butter, garlic, herbs, salt, and pepper.
3. Rub mixture over chicken.
4. Place on roasting pan, tie legs.
5. Roast until golden and cooked.
6. Let rest, carve.
7. Serve with lemon wedges.
8. Savor the roasted perfection.

Substitutions

Any type of fresh herbs

4 servings

360 cal

2 hours

Coq au Vin Blanc

Ingredients:

- 4 chicken legs (bone-in and skin-on)
- 1 cup white wine
- 1 cup chicken broth
- 1 cup mushrooms (sliced)
- 8 shallots (peeled and halved)
- 1/4 cup all-purpose flour
- 1/4 cup butter
- Fresh thyme sprigs
vSalt and pepper to taste

Substitutions

Any type of mushrooms

A white wine twist on a classic—Coq au Vin Blanc. This dish features tender chicken cooked in white wine with mushrooms and shallots. With each bite, you're savoring the delicate flavors and richness of French comfort.

Directions

1. Season chicken with salt and pepper.
2. Dredge in flour, shake off excess.
3. Heat butter, brown chicken.
4. Remove chicken from pan.
5. Sauté mushrooms and shallots.
6. Deglaze with wine, reduce.
7. Add chicken broth, thyme.
8. Return chicken to pan, simmer.
9. Savor the white wine delight.

6
servings

320 cal

2 hours

Chicken and Leek Pie

Ingredients:

- 1 pie crust
- 2 cups cooked chicken (cubed)
- 2 leeks (cleaned and sliced)
- 1/4 cup butter
- 1/4 cup all-purpose flour
- 1 1/2 cups chicken broth
- 1/2 cup heavy cream
- Salt and pepper to taste
- Fresh parsley (for garnish)

Substitutions

Any type of cooked meat

A savory pie with rustic charm—Chicken and Leek Pie. This dish features tender chicken and sautéed leeks in a flaky crust. With each bite, you're savoring the simple elegance of French country cooking.

Directions

1. Preheat oven.
2. Melt butter, sauté leeks.
3. Stir in flour, cook until bubbly.
4. Add broth, cream, seasonings.
5. Simmer until thickened.
6. Stir in chicken.
7. Pour filling into pie crust.
8. Top with another pie crust.
9. Bake until golden and bubbling.
10. Garnish with parsley.
11. Savor the rustic goodness.

4
servings

380 cal

1.5
hours

Chicken Cordon Bleu

Ingredients:

- 4 chicken breasts (boneless and skinless)
- 4 slices ham
- 4 slices Swiss cheese
- 1/2 cup all-purpose flour
- 2 eggs
- 1 cup breadcrumbs
- Butter (for cooking)
- Salt and pepper to taste

An elegant twist on chicken—Chicken Cordon Bleu. This dish features tender chicken stuffed with ham and cheese, coated in breadcrumbs. With each bite, you're savoring the harmonious blend of flavors and textures.

Directions

1. Preheat oven.
2. Flatten chicken breasts, season.
3. Place ham and cheese on each breast.
4. Roll up, secure with toothpicks.
5. Dredge in flour, shake off excess.
6. Dip in beaten eggs.
7. Coat with breadcrumbs.
8. Heat butter, brown chicken.
9. Transfer to oven, bake until cooked.
10. Savor the indulgent delight.

Substitutions

Any type of cheese, any type of cooked meat

4 servings

280 cal

1.5 hours

Chicken and Chive Crêpes

Ingredients:

- 1 cup all-purpose flour
- 2 eggs, 1 1/4 cups milk
- 2 tbsp butter (melted)
- Salt to taste, Butter (for cooking)
- 2 cups cooked chicken (shredded)
- 1/4 cup chives (chopped)
- 1/2 cup béchamel sauce

A delicate French treat—Chicken and Chive Crêpes. These tender crêpes are filled with chicken and chives, creating a harmonious blend of flavors. With each bite, you're savoring the elegant simplicity of French cuisine.

Directions

1. Blend flour, eggs, milk, and melted butter.
2. Heat pan, make crêpes.
3. Mix chicken, chives, and béchamel.
4. Fill crêpes with mixture.
5. Fold and warm.
6. Savor the delicate delight.

Substitutions

Any type of cooked meat, any type of herbs

Chapter 9:
Nourishing
Seafood Creations

4 servings

250 cal

30 min

Moules Marinières (Mussels in White Wine)

Ingredients:

- 2 lbs mussels (cleaned and debearded)
- 1/4 cup butter
- 1/2 cup shallots (chopped)
- 2 cloves garlic (minced)
- 1 cup white wine
- 1/2 cup heavy cream
- Fresh parsley (for garnish)
- Crusty bread (for dipping)

A taste of the sea kissed by wine—Moules Marinières. This dish features plump mussels in a fragrant white wine broth. With each bite, you're savoring the briny delight and elegance of coastal cuisine.

Directions

1. Melt butter, sauté shallots and garlic.
2. Add wine, simmer.
3. Add mussels, cover, steam until opened.
4. Stir in cream, simmer.
5. Garnish with parsley.
6. Serve with crusty bread.
7. Savor the coastal elegance.

Substitutions

Any type of wine

4
servings

280 cal

25 min

Sole Meunière

Ingredients:

- 4 sole fillets
- 1/4 cup all-purpose flour
- Salt and pepper to taste
- 1/4 cup butter
- Juice of 1 lemon
- Fresh parsley (for garnish)

A delicate fish with buttery charm—Sole Meunière. This dish features tender sole fish cooked in butter and lemon. With each bite, you're experiencing the refined simplicity and delicate flavors of French seafood.

Directions

1. Season fish with salt and pepper.
2. Dredge in flour, shake off excess.
3. Heat butter in pan.
4. Cook fish until golden and cooked.
5. Squeeze lemon juice over fish.
6. Garnish with parsley.
7. Savor the delicate delight.

Substitutions

Any type of fish fillets

4 servings | **220 cal** | **40 min**

Boulettes de Poisson (Fish Balls)

Ingredients:

- 1 lb white fish fillets
- 1/4 cup onions (chopped)
- 2 cloves garlic (minced)
- 1/4 cup fresh herbs (parsley, dill, chives)
- 1/4 cup breadcrumbs
- 1 egg, Salt and pepper to taste
- 1/4 cup flour, Butter (for cooking)
- Lemon wedges (for serving)

A playful seafood treat—Boulettes de Poisson. These fish balls are flavored with herbs and spices, creating a savory delight. With each bite, you're savoring the unique texture and flavors of French seafood.

Directions

1. Blend fish, onions, garlic, herbs.
2. Mix in breadcrumbs, egg, seasonings.
3. Shape into balls, coat with flour.
4. Heat butter in pan.
5. Cook fish balls until golden and cooked.
6. Serve with lemon wedges.
7. Savor the playful delight.

Substitutions

Any type of herbs

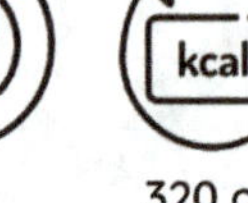

4
servings

320 cal

1.5
hours

Salmon en Croûte

Ingredients:

- 4 salmon fillets
- 1 sheet puff pastry
- 1/4 cup Dijon mustard
- Salt and pepper to taste
- 1 egg (beaten, for egg wash)
- Fresh dill (for garnish)

A regal dish in pastry—Salmon en Croûte. This creation features succulent salmon fillets encased in flaky puff pastry. With each bite, you're savoring the richness and elegance of French seafood presentation.

Directions

1. Preheat oven.
2. Season salmon with salt and pepper.
3. Spread mustard on fillets.
4. Roll out and cut puff pastry.
5. Place salmon on pastry, wrap.
6. Brush with egg wash.
7. Bake until golden and cooked.
8. Garnish with dill.
9. Savor the regal presentation.

Substitutions

Any type of mustard

6 servings

280 cal

1.5 hours

Seafood Gratin

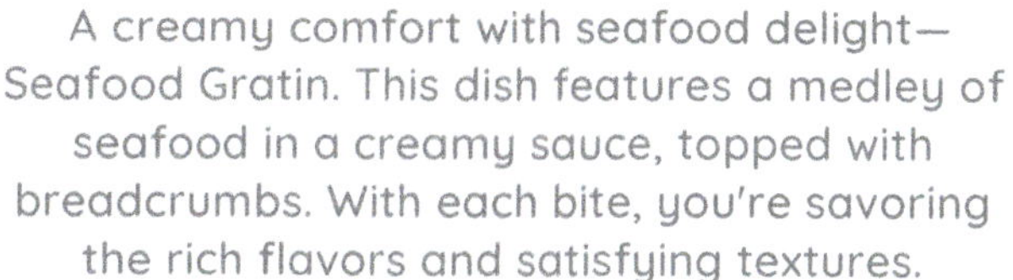

Ingredients:

- 1 cup mixed seafood (shrimp, scallops, fish)
- 1/4 cup butter
- 1/4 cup all-purpose flour
- 1 1/2 cups milk
- 1/2 cup heavy cream
- 1/4 cup grated Gruyère cheese
- Salt and pepper to taste
- Breadcrumbs (for topping)
- Fresh herbs (for garnish)

Substitutions

Any type of seafood

A creamy comfort with seafood delight—Seafood Gratin. This dish features a medley of seafood in a creamy sauce, topped with breadcrumbs. With each bite, you're savoring the rich flavors and satisfying textures.

Directions

1. Melt butter, stir in flour.
2. Add milk, cream, seasonings.
3. Stir in seafood and cheese.
4. Transfer to baking dish.
5. Top with breadcrumbs.
6. Bake until bubbly and golden.
7. Garnish with herbs.
8. Savor the creamy comfort.

4
servings

320 cal

30 min

Shrimp Scampi

Ingredients:

- 1 lb large shrimp (peeled and deveined),
1/4 cup butter
- 4 cloves garlic (minced)
- 1/2 cup white wine, Juice of 1 lemon, Red
pepper flakes (optional)
- Fresh parsley (for garnish)
- Linguine or crusty bread (for serving)

A garlicky delight from the sea—Shrimp Scampi. This dish features plump shrimp sautéed in a fragrant garlic and white wine sauce. With each bite, you're savoring the vibrant flavors and succulent texture of seafood.

Directions

1. Heat butter, sauté garlic.
2. Add shrimp, cook until pink.
3. Deglaze with wine, reduce.
4. Squeeze lemon juice, add pepper flakes.
5. Serve over linguine or with crusty bread.
6. Garnish with parsley.
7. Savor the garlicky delight.

Substitutions

Any type of wine

 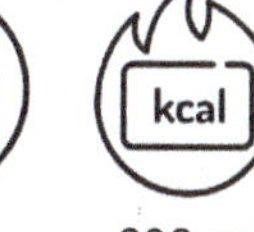 

4
servings

280 cal

1.5
hours

Fisherman's Stew (Matelote)

Ingredients:

- 1 lb mixed fish (cod, trout, salmon)
- 1/4 cup butter
- 1/2 cup onions (chopped)
- 1/4 cup carrots (chopped)
- 1/4 cup celery (chopped)
- 1/4 cup all-purpose flour
- 1 cup red wine
- 1 cup fish broth
- 1/4 cup heavy cream
- Fresh parsley (for garnish)
- Crusty bread (for serving)

Substitutions

Any type of wine

A hearty fisherman's delight—Fisherman's Stew. This dish features fish and vegetables simmered in a rich wine-infused broth. With each bite, you're savoring the rustic flavors and heartiness of French coastal cuisine.

Directions

1. Melt butter, sauté onions, carrots, celery.
2. Stir in flour, cook until bubbly.
3. Add wine, fish broth, seasonings.
4. Simmer until vegetables are tender.
5. Add fish, cream, simmer.
6. Garnish with parsley.
7. Serve with crusty bread.
8. Savor the hearty stew.

4
servings

280 cal

30 min

Tuna Niçoise Salad

Ingredients:

- 2 tuna steaks
- 4 cups mixed greens
- 4 hard-boiled eggs (quartered)
- 1/2 cup cherry tomatoes
- 1/4 cup black olives
- 1/4 cup green beans (blanched)
- 2 tbsp capers
- 1/4 cup red onion (sliced)
- Lemon vinaigrette (olive oil, lemon juice, Dijon mustard, salt, pepper)

A Mediterranean escape on a plate—Tuna Niçoise Salad. This salad features seared tuna, fresh vegetables, and briny olives, creating a balanced and satisfying dish. With each bite, you're savoring the vibrant flavors and textures of coastal France.

Directions

1. Season tuna, sear until desired doneness.
2. Arrange greens on plates.
3. Arrange tuna, eggs, tomatoes, olives, beans, capers, onion.
4. Drizzle with lemon vinaigrette.
5. Savor the Mediterranean escape.

Substitutions

Any type of fish steak

**6
servings**

340 cal

**1.5
hours**

Seafood Quiche

Ingredients:

- 1 pie crust
- 1 cup mixed seafood (shrimp, crab, scallops)
- 1/4 cup green onions (chopped)
- 1/4 cup fresh herbs (parsley, dill)
- 4 eggs, 1 cup milk
- Salt and pepper to taste
- 1/4 cup grated Gruyère cheese

A savory delight in every slice—Seafood Quiche. This quiche features a mix of seafood and herbs in a delicate custard, all nestled in a buttery crust. With each bite, you're savoring the harmonious blend of flavors and textures.

Directions

1. Preheat oven.
2. Sauté seafood, green onions, herbs.
3. Mix eggs, milk, salt, and pepper.
4. Place seafood mixture in pie crust.
5. Pour egg mixture over.
6. Sprinkle with cheese.
7. Bake until set and golden.
8. Savor the savory slice.

Substitutions

Any type of seafood

4
servings

280 cal

1.5
hours

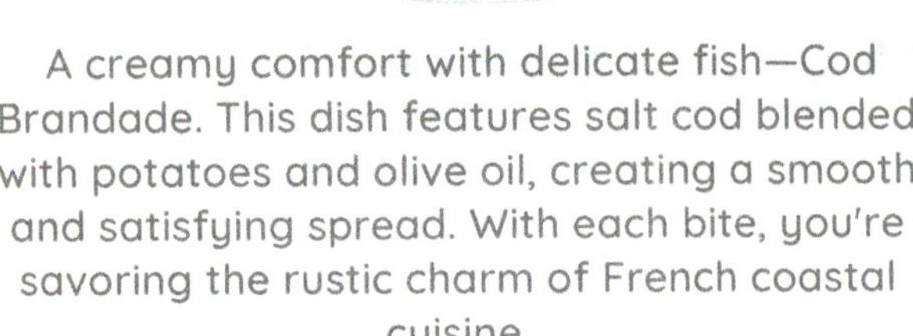

Cod Brandade

Ingredients:

- 1/2 lb salt cod
- 2 cups potatoes (peeled and diced)
- 1/4 cup olive oil
- 2 cloves garlic (minced)
- 1/4 cup milk
- Salt and pepper to taste
- Fresh parsley (for garnish)
- Crusty bread (for serving)

A creamy comfort with delicate fish—Cod Brandade. This dish features salt cod blended with potatoes and olive oil, creating a smooth and satisfying spread. With each bite, you're savoring the rustic charm of French coastal cuisine.

Directions

1. Soak salt cod, change water.
2. Boil cod and potatoes, drain.
3. Purée cod, potatoes, garlic.
4. Add olive oil, milk, seasonings.
5. Garnish with parsley.
6. Serve with crusty bread.
7. Savor the creamy delight.

Substitutions

Any type of fish

Chapter 10:
Cheese Delights
and Savory Tarts

6 servings

320 cal

1.5 hours

Quiche aux Fromages (Cheese Quiche)

Ingredients:

- 1 pie crust
- 1 cup mixed cheeses (Gruyère, Cheddar, Emmental)
- 4 eggs
- 1 1/2 cups milk
- Salt and pepper to taste
- Fresh herbs (for garnish)

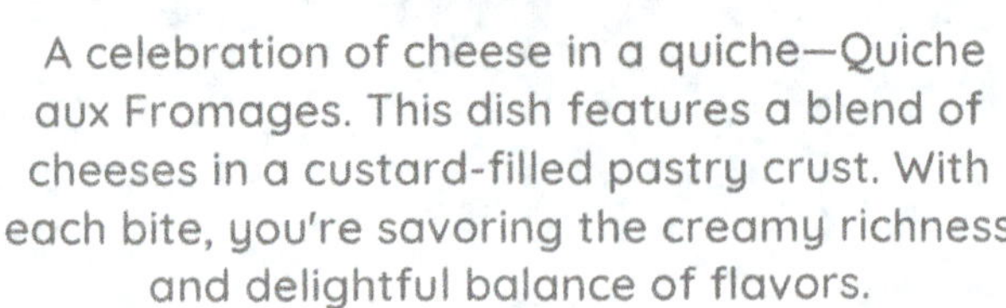

A celebration of cheese in a quiche—Quiche aux Fromages. This dish features a blend of cheeses in a custard-filled pastry crust. With each bite, you're savoring the creamy richness and delightful balance of flavors.

Directions

1. Preheat oven.
2. Sprinkle cheese over pie crust.
3. Whisk eggs, milk, salt, and pepper.
4. Pour mixture over cheese.
5. Bake until set and golden.
6. Garnish with fresh herbs.
7. Savor the cheesy delight.

Substitutions

Any type of mixed cheeses

4 servings

360 cal

30 min

Croque-Madame

Ingredients:

- 8 slices sandwich bread
- 8 slices ham
- 1 1/2 cups grated Gruyère cheese
- 4 eggs
- 1/4 cup butter
- Salt and pepper to taste
- Dijon mustard (for spreading)

A hearty sandwich with a fried twist—Croque-Madame. This dish features a ham and cheese sandwich topped with a sunny-side-up egg. With each bite, you're savoring the comforting flavors and satisfying textures.

Directions

1. Preheat oven.
2. Assemble sandwiches with ham and cheese.
3. Spread mustard, top with more cheese.
4. Melt butter, toast sandwiches until golden.
5. Fry eggs, sunny-side-up.
6. Place eggs on top of sandwiches.
7. Bake until cheese is bubbly.
8. Savor the hearty sandwich.

Substitutions

Any type of ham, any type of cheese

4 servings

300 cal

1.5 hours

Tarte Flambée (Alsatian Pizza)

Ingredients:

- 1 pre-made pizza dough
- 1 cup fromage blanc
- 1 cup onions (thinly sliced)
- 1/2 cup bacon (thinly sliced)
- Fresh thyme leaves
- Salt and pepper to taste

A unique pizza with French flair—Tarte Flambée. This dish features a thin crust topped with fromage blanc, onions, and bacon. With each bite, you're savoring the distinctive flavors and regional charm.

Directions

1. Preheat oven with pizza stone.
2. Roll out dough, spread fromage blanc.
3. Top with onions and bacon.
4. Sprinkle with thyme, salt, and pepper.
5. Transfer to pizza stone, bake until crust is crisp.
6. Savor the Alsatian twist.

Substitutions

Any type of soft cheese

4 servings

340 cal

1.5 hours

Cheese Soufflé

Ingredients:

- 1/4 cup butter
- 1/4 cup all-purpose flour
- 1 1/2 cups milk
- 1 1/2 cups grated Gruyère cheese
- 4 egg yolks
- 4 egg whites
- Salt and pepper to taste
- Nutmeg (for flavor)
- Fresh herbs (for garnish)

An elegant rise of cheesy delight—Cheese Soufflé. This dish features a fluffy soufflé infused with cheese and baked to perfection. With each bite, you're savoring the airy texture and savory richness of French cuisine.

Directions

1. Preheat oven.
2. Melt butter, stir in flour.
3. Add milk, whisk until thickened.
4. Stir in cheese, egg yolks, seasonings.
5. Whip egg whites until stiff peaks form.
6. Gently fold egg whites into cheese mixture.
7. Transfer to ramekins, bake until puffed and golden.
8. Garnish with herbs.
9. Savor the airy delight.

Substitutions

Any type of cheese

 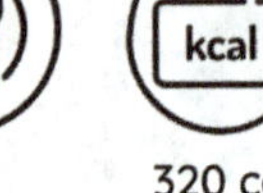 

6 servings

320 cal

1.5 hours

Gruyère and Caramelized Onion Tart

Ingredients:

- 1 pre-made pie crust
- 4 cups onions (thinly sliced)
- 2 tbsp butter
- 1 cup grated Gruyère cheese
- 2 eggs
- 1 cup heavy cream
- Salt and pepper to taste
- Fresh thyme leaves (for garnish)

A symphony of flavors in a savory tart—Gruyère and Caramelized Onion Tart. This dish features sweet caramelized onions and Gruyère cheese in a buttery pastry crust. With each bite, you're savoring the balance of sweet and savory.

Directions

1. Preheat oven.
2. Sauté onions in butter until caramelized.
3. Line pie crust with caramelized onions.
4. Sprinkle with cheese.
5. Mix eggs, cream, salt, and pepper.
6. Pour mixture over onions and cheese.
7. Bake until set and golden.
8. Garnish with thyme.
9. Savor the symphony of flavors.

Substitutions

Any type of cheese

4 servings

280 cal

40 min

Roquefort-Stuffed Pears

Ingredients:

- 4 pears (firm and ripe)
- 1/2 cup Roquefort cheese (crumbled)
- 1/4 cup honey
- 1/4 cup walnuts (chopped)
- Fresh thyme leaves (for garnish)

A delectable fusion of sweet and savory—Roquefort-Stuffed Pears. This dish features pears filled with Roquefort cheese and honey, creating a harmonious blend of flavors. With each bite, you're savoring the delightful contrast and elegance.

Directions

1. Preheat oven.
2. Cut pears in half, core.
3. Mix Roquefort, honey, walnuts.
4. Fill pear halves with mixture.
5. Bake until pears are tender and cheese is melted.
6. Garnish with thyme.
7. Savor the sweet-savory delight.

Substitutions

Any type of blue cheese

4
servings

380 cal

1.5
hours

Tartiflette

Ingredients:

- 2 lbs potatoes (peeled and sliced)
- 1/2 lb bacon (diced)
- 1 onion (sliced)
v1/2 cup dry white wine
- 1/2 cup heavy cream
- 1 Reblochon cheese
Salt and pepper to taste

A hearty Alpine indulgence—Tartiflette. This dish features layers of potatoes, Reblochon cheese, and bacon, all baked to creamy perfection. With each bite, you're savoring the rich flavors and comforting warmth of Alpine cuisine.

Directions

1. Preheat oven.
2. Boil potatoes until tender.
3. Sauté bacon and onion.
4. Add wine, reduce.
5. Layer potatoes, bacon, and cheese in baking dish.
6. Pour cream over.
7. Bake until cheese is melted and bubbly.
8. Savor the Alpine indulgence.

Substitutions

Any type of cheese, any type of bacon

4
servings

360 cal

40 min

Three-Cheese Fondue

Ingredients:

- 1 cup Gruyère cheese (grated)
- 1 cup Emmental cheese (grated)
- 1 cup Comté cheese (grated)
- 2 cups dry white wine
- 1 clove garlic (cut in half)
- 1 tbsp lemon juice, Nutmeg (for flavor)
- Cubes of crusty bread
- Vegetables for dipping

A communal dip of cheesy delight—Three-Cheese Fondue. This dish features a blend of cheeses melted in white wine, perfect for dipping bread and vegetables. With each bite, you're savoring the interactive and indulgent experience.

Directions

1. Rub pot with garlic, discard.
2. Heat wine in pot.
3. Gradually add cheeses, stir until melted.
4. Stir in lemon juice, nutmeg.
5. Serve with bread and vegetables.
6. Savor the communal dip.

Substitutions

Any type of cheese

4
servings

320 cal

40 min

Camembert Baked in Pastry

Ingredients:

- 1 wheel Camembert cheese
- 1 sheet puff pastry
- 1 egg (beaten, for egg wash)
- Honey (for drizzling)
- Fresh rosemary (for garnish)
- Sliced baguette (for serving)

Substitutions

Any type of soft cheese

A warm embrace of cheese and pastry—Camembert Baked in Pastry. This dish features a whole Camembert cheese wrapped in flaky pastry and baked to gooey perfection. With each bite, you're savoring the melty richness and indulgent warmth.

Directions

1. Preheat oven.
2. Roll out puff pastry.
3. Place Camembert in center.
4. Wrap with pastry, seal edges.
5. Brush with egg wash.
6. Bake until golden and cheese is gooey.
7. Drizzle with honey, garnish with rosemary.
8. Serve with baguette slices.
9. Savor the gooey embrace.

4
servings

280 cal

25 min

Endive and Blue Cheese Salad

Ingredients:

- 4 endives (trimmed and separated into leaves)
- 1/2 cup blue cheese (crumbled)
- 1/4 cup walnuts (chopped)
- 1/4 cup olive oil
- 2 tbsp red wine vinegar
- Dijon mustard
- Salt and pepper to taste

A tangy and crisp salad—Endive and Blue Cheese Salad. This dish features endive leaves topped with blue cheese, walnuts, and a zesty vinaigrette. With each bite, you're savoring the refreshing crunch and bold flavors.

Directions

1. Arrange endive leaves on plates.
2. Sprinkle with blue cheese and walnuts.
3. Whisk olive oil, vinegar, mustard, salt, and pepper.
4. Drizzle vinaigrette over salad.
5. Savor the tangy and crisp bite.

Substitutions

Any type of blue cheese

Chapter 11:
Sweet Confections and Treats

4
servings

280 cal

1.5
hours

Crème Caramel

Ingredients:

- 1/2 cup sugar
- 2 tbsp water
- 2 cups milk
- 4 eggs
- 1/2 cup sugar (for custard)
- 1 tsp vanilla extract
- Pinch of salt

Substitutions

Any type of milk, any type of sugar

A silky masterpiece of caramel—Crème Caramel. This dessert features smooth custard topped with a luscious caramel sauce. With each bite, you're savoring the elegant balance of flavors and textures.

Directions

1. Preheat oven.
2. Make caramel by melting sugar and water.
3. Pour caramel into ramekins.
4. Heat milk until scalded.
5. Whisk eggs, sugar, vanilla, and salt.
6. Gradually add milk, whisk.
7. Pour mixture over caramel.
8. Bake in water bath until set.
9. Chill, invert, and savor.

**4
servings**

320 cal

**1.5
hours**

Pots de Crème

Ingredients:

- 1 cup heavy cream
- 1/2 cup milk
- 4 oz bittersweet chocolate (chopped)
- 4 egg yolks
- 1/4 cup sugar
- 1 tsp vanilla extract
- Pinch of salt

A velvety delight in a pot—Pots de Crème. This dessert features rich chocolate custard baked to perfection. With each bite, you're savoring the smoothness and depth of flavor that only chocolate can bring.

Directions

1. Preheat oven.
2. Heat cream and milk, add chocolate.
3. Whisk egg yolks, sugar, vanilla, and salt.
4. Gradually add cream mixture, whisk.
5. Strain mixture, divide into ramekins.
6. Bake in water bath until set.
7. Chill, savor the velvety treat.

Substitutions

Any type of chocolate

20 macarons

150 cal

2 hours

Raspberry Macarons

Ingredients:

- 1 cup almond flour
- 1 3/4 cups powdered sugar
- 3 large egg whites
v1/4 cup granulated sugar
- Pink food coloring
- 1/2 cup butter
- 1 cup powdered sugar
- 1/4 cup raspberry jam

A delicate embrace of raspberry—Raspberry Macarons. These confections feature almond meringue shells filled with raspberry buttercream. With each bite, you're savoring the airy crunch and fruity sweetness.

Directions

1. Preheat oven.
2. Pulse almond flour and powdered sugar.
3. Beat egg whites, gradually add granulated sugar.
4. Fold in almond mixture, add food coloring.
5. Pipe onto baking sheets, rest.
6. Bake until set and feet form.
7. Beat butter, powdered sugar, and jam.
8. Fill macarons with buttercream.
9. Savor the delicate crunch.

Substitutions

Any type of jam

4
servings

340 cal

2 hours

Mille-Feuille

Ingredients:

- 1 sheet puff pastry
- 2 cups milk
- 4 egg yolks
- 1/2 cup sugar
- 1/4 cup cornstarch
- 1 tsp vanilla extract
- Powdered sugar (for dusting)

A thousand layers of delight—Mille-Feuille. This dessert features layers of flaky pastry filled with pastry cream. With each bite, you're savoring the exquisite blend of textures and flavors.

Directions

1. Preheat oven.
2. Roll out puff pastry, bake until golden.
3. Heat milk until scalded.
4. Whisk egg yolks, sugar, and cornstarch.
5. Gradually add milk, whisk.
6. Return to heat, cook until thickened.
7. Stir in vanilla.
8. Assemble layers of pastry and cream.
9. Dust with powdered sugar.
10. Savor the layers of delight.

Substitutions

Any type of milk, any type of sugar

20 cream puffs

180 cal

1.5 hours

Choux à la Crème (Cream Puffs)

Ingredients:

- 1/2 cup butter
- 1 cup water
- 1 cup all-purpose flour
- 4 eggs
- 2 cups milk
- 4 egg yolks
- 1/2 cup sugar
- 1/4 cup cornstarch
- 1 tsp vanilla extract

Substitutions

Any type of milk, any type of sugar

A bite-sized cloud of cream—Choux à la Crème. These puffs feature airy pastry shells filled with vanilla pastry cream. With each bite, you're savoring the delicate balance of textures and sweetness.

Directions

1. Preheat oven.
2. Boil butter and water.
3. Stir in flour, cook until smooth.
4. Beat in eggs one at a time.
5. Pipe onto baking sheets, bake until puffed.
6. Heat milk until scalded.
7. Whisk egg yolks, sugar, and cornstarch.
8. Gradually add milk, whisk.
9. Return to heat, cook until thickened.
10. Stir in vanilla.
11. Fill puffs with cream.
12. Savor the airy delight.

20 pieces **160 cal** **2 hours**

Nougat

Ingredients:

- 1 1/2 cups mixed nuts (almonds, pistachios, hazelnuts)
- 1 1/4 cups sugar
- 1/2 cup honey
- 2 egg whites
- 1/4 tsp vanilla extract

A chewy delight of nuts and honey—Nougat. This confection features a blend of nuts, honey, and egg whites. With each bite, you're savoring the chewy texture and nutty sweetness.

Directions

1. Toast nuts, chop roughly.
2. Line pan with parchment paper.
3. Heat sugar and honey until dissolved.
4. Beat egg whites until stiff peaks form.
5. Gradually add sugar mixture, beat until cool and glossy.
6. Fold in nuts and vanilla.
7. Spread mixture in pan, let set.
8. Cut into pieces, savor the chewy delight.

Substitutions

Any type of nuts

20 calissons

130 cal

2 hours

Calissons

Ingredients:

- 1 cup almond flour
- 1/2 cup powdered sugar
- 1/4 cup candied fruit (orange, melon)
- 1/4 cup ground blanched almonds
- 1/4 cup honey
- 1/4 tsp almond extract
- 1 egg white
- 1 1/2 cups powdered sugar (for icing)
- Food coloring (optional)

A confection of almond and candied fruit—Calissons. These treats feature a marzipan-like base topped with a layer of royal icing. With each bite, you're savoring the tender almond sweetness and slight crunch.

Directions

1. Pulse almond flour, powdered sugar, candied fruit.
2. Add ground almonds, honey, and almond extract.
3. Beat egg white, fold into almond mixture.
4. Roll out dough, cut shapes.
5. Let dry for a day.
6. Mix powdered sugar, water, and food coloring.
7. Spread icing on shapes.
8. Savor the tender delight.

Substitutions

Any type of candied fruit

6 servings

340 cal

1.5 hours

Walnut Tart

Ingredients:

- 1 pre-made pie crust
- 2 cups walnuts (chopped)
- 3/4 cup brown sugar
- 1/4 cup honey
- 3 eggs
- 1/4 cup butter (melted)
- 1 tsp vanilla extract

A nutty indulgence in a crust—Walnut Tart. This dessert features a filling of walnuts in a buttery pastry crust. With each bite, you're savoring the rich nuttiness and comforting sweetness.

Directions

1. Preheat oven.
2. Roll out pie crust, place in pan.
3. Mix walnuts, brown sugar, honey.
4. Beat eggs, add butter and vanilla.
5. Mix wet and dry ingredients.
6. Pour mixture into crust.
7. Bake until filling is set.
8. Savor the nutty indulgence.

Substitutions

Any type of nuts

20 truffles

180 cal

2 hours

Walnut Tart

Ingredients:

- 8 oz bittersweet chocolate (chopped)
- 1/2 cup heavy cream
- 2 tbsp butter
- Cocoa powder (for rolling)

A luxurious bite of chocolate—Chocolate Truffles. These treats feature ganache rolled in cocoa powder. With each bite, you're savoring the velvety chocolate richness and elegant finish.

Directions

1. Heat cream, pour over chocolate and butter.
2. Stir until smooth.
3. Chill until firm.
4. Scoop, roll into balls.
5. Roll in cocoa powder.
6. Savor the luxurious bite.

Substitutions

Any type of chocolate

 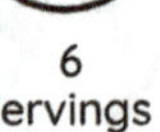  

6
servings

320 cal

1.5
hours

Tarte aux Pommes (French Apple Tart)

Ingredients:

- 1 pre-made pie crust
- 4 apples (peeled, cored, sliced)
- 1/4 cup apricot jam (warmed)
- 2 tbsp butter (melted)
- 2 tbsp sugar
- Cinnamon (for sprinkling)

A classic beauty of apples and pastry—Tarte aux Pommes. This dessert features a ring of sliced apples on a buttery pastry crust. With each bite, you're savoring the comforting flavors and timeless elegance.

Directions

1. Preheat oven.
2. Roll out pie crust, place in pan.
3. Arrange apple slices in a ring.
4. Brush with melted butter.
5. Sprinkle with sugar and cinnamon.
6. Bake until apples are tender.
7. Brush with warmed apricot jam.
8. Savor the classic beauty.

Substitutions

Any type of apples

We need your help

As we reach the end of this culinary journey we'd like to ask for your support. Reviews are indeed hard to come by, and if you've enjoyed this book and found our recipes delightful, we kindly request that you take a moment to share your thoughts.

Please go back to your app or the platform where you made your purchase, click on the review button, and give us a rating along with a short sentence about your experience. Your feedback means the world to us.

Being a small publisher, reviews are a precious resource that can make a significant difference for us. Your review could help us drastically in reaching more readers who share your passion for New England comfort cuisine.

Rest assured, we read and appreciate every single review, and your input is invaluable to us. If you happen to come across any small mistakes, please understand that we've done our best to provide you with an exceptional cookbook. However, as in any creative endeavor, sometimes mistakes can slip through. We hope you can overlook them and focus on the love and dedication that went into every recipe.